God, ethics and the human genome

God, ethics and the human genome

Theological, legal and scientific perspectives

Edited by Mark Bratton
on behalf of the Mission and Public Affairs Council of the
Church of England

CHURCH HOUSE
PUBLISHING

Church House Publishing
Church House
Great Smith Street
London SW1P 3AZ

Tel: 020 7898 1451
Fax: 020 7898 1449

ISBN 978 0 7151 4139 7

GS Misc 917

Published 2009 by Church House Publishing

The opinions expressed in this book are those of the individual authors
and do not necessarily reflect the official policy of the General Synod
or The Archbishops' Council of the Church of England.

The Scripture quotations contained herein are from the New Revised Standard
Version of the Bible, Anglicized Edition, copyright © 1989, 1995 by the
Division of Christian Education of the National Council of the Churches
of Christ in the United States of America, and are used by permission.
All rights reserved.

Typeset in 9.5pt Stone Sans
by RefineCatch Limited, Bungay, Suffolk
Printed by Ashford Colour Press Ltd, Fareham, Hants

PEFC
PEFC/16-33-366

Contents

Contributors

The Revd Professor Nigel Biggar is Regius Professor of Moral and Pastoral Theology at the University of Oxford. He sits on the Royal College of Physicians' Committee for Ethical Issues in Medicine, and he is the author of *Aiming to Kill: The Ethics of Suicide and Euthanasia* (Darton, Longman & Todd, 2004). He is currently writing a book on the proper nature of theological contributions to public debate.

The Revd Mark Bratton, a former practising barrister, is Senior Chaplain at the University of Warwick and Area Dean of Coventry (South). He is also an honorary lecturer in values-in-medicine in the Medical School at the University of Warwick and vice-chairman of the Coventry Research Ethics Committee. He has written on a range of topics within bioethics and medical law, including most recently *The Human Genome Project* (Grove Series, 2008). He is a member of the General Synod of the Church of England, representing Coventry, and also a member of its Mission and Public Affairs Council.

The Revd Dr Malcolm Brown is Director of Mission and Public Affairs for the Archbishops' Council of the Church of England. He was formerly principal of the Eastern Region Ministry Course in Cambridge, where he taught Christian Ethics, and executive secretary of the William Temple Foundation in Manchester, where he ran programmes examining the churches' involvement in public affairs and economic issues in Britain and Europe. His main areas of academic interest are the challenges which Christian ethics poses to the liberal foundations of market economics and the problems of Christian engagement with public affairs in a consumer society.

Dr Donald Bruce holds doctorates in chemistry and in theology and has a wide expertise in ethical issues in GM crops and animals, cloning and stem cells, environment, and nanotechnologies. He formerly worked in nuclear waste research and risk assessment from 1976 to 1992. From 1992 to 2007 he was director of the Church of Scotland's Society, Religion and Technology Project, and is now managing director of the consultancy company, Edinethics

Ltd. He has examined and spoken on ethical issues of biotechnology patenting since 1993, and drafted the position papers of the Conference of European Churches and Church of Scotland. He is currently a member of the Societal Issues Panel of the UK Engineering and Physical Sciences Research Council, and formerly of the Scottish Science Advisory Committee.

Professor Annette Cashmore is director of GENIE Centre for Excellence in Teaching and Learning in Genetics and sub-dean in the Faculty of Medicine and Biological Sciences at the University of Leicester. In 2002 Annette led the successful bid for the prestigious Queen's Anniversary Prize for Further and Higher Education awarded for both the scientific achievements of the Genetics Department at the University of Leicester as well as work to engage with the public. In 2008, she was made a National Teaching Fellow for excellence in higher education teaching. She serves on several national committees influencing policy on science and medical education and combines her teaching and leadership roles with running a successful research group working on the pathogenic fungus *Candida albicans*. She is also a lay-member of Chapter at Leicester Cathedral.

Dr Sue Chetwynd is an associate fellow of the University of Warwick. She is a philosopher by training who specializes in professional ethics. At present she is based in the Engineering Department at Warwick, where she teaches professional ethics to undergraduates, and is a member of the Teaching Engineering Ethics Group of the Royal Academy of Engineering. She also teaches medical ethics at Leicester and Warwick Medical Schools, both at undergraduate level and on continuing professional development modules, and keeps her philosophical eye in by tutoring for the Warwick Philosophy Department on a variety of modules.

The Revd Professor Michael Northcott is Professor of Ethics in the School of Divinity in the University of Edinburgh and a priest in the Scottish Episcopal Church. He is the author of many books and papers on environmental theology and ethics. His most recent books are *A Moral Climate: The Ethics of Global Warming* (Darton, Longman & Todd, 2007) and *Diversity and Dominion: Science Ethics and Nature*, edited with Kyle Vanhoutan (Duke University Press, 2009).

Mr John Overton retired in September 2008 after working for 30 years as a patent attorney with a major multinational company, the last 10 years as head of its London patents division. For the last ten years he represented his employer on the Council of the Trade Marks, Patents and Designs Federation (TMPDF), an organization which was founded in 1920 in order to coordinate the views of industry and commerce in the UK, and to make representations to the appropriate authorities on policy and practice in intellectual property matters. He is a member of Oxford Diocesan Synod.

Dr Peter Manley Scott is Senior Lecturer in Christian Social Thought and Director of the Lincoln Theological Institute at the University of Manchester, UK. He is author of *Theology, Ideology and Liberation* (Cambridge University Press, 1994; paperback edition 2008) and *A Political Theology of Nature* (Cambridge University Press, 2003); co-editor of *The Blackwell Companion to Political Theology* (Blackwell, 2004; paperback edition 2006), *Future Perfect* (Continuum, 2006), *Re-moralising Britain?* (Continuum, 2009), *Nature Space and the Sacred* (Ashgate 2009); and guest editor of *Ecotheology* 11.2, a – special issue on theology and technology (Equinox, 2006), and the *International Journal of Public Theology* 2.1, a – special issue on urban theology (Brill, 2008).

Dr Robert Song is Senior Lecturer in Christian Ethics at the University of Durham, and is the author of *Christianity and Liberal Society* (Clarendon Press, 1997) and *Human Genetics: Fabricating the Future* (Darton, Longman & Todd, 2001), and many articles in Christian ethics and political thought. His current research is on the theological foundations of bioethics. He is reviews editor for *Studies in Christian Ethics*, and also chairs the Epiphany Trust, which provides holidays for adults with learning disabilities in Britain and abroad.

Foreword

Bishop David Sheppard when Chair of the Church of England's Board for Social Responsibility used to speak of the importance of 'shining the light of the gospel' on the issues of the day. I doubt whether he had the possible patenting of the human genome in mind at the time but the point he wanted to underline was that it is the responsibility of Christians to show how our Christian faith and understanding impacts the whole range of issues that affect human life and society. We may think patenting is a narrow aspect of the law and the term 'human genome' an obscure scientific technical term. But as the contributions to this book so clearly show, the issues surrounding them are of vital importance to our society and the future of humankind. We who are Christians therefore have a responsibility to address them and show how our understanding of the lordship of Jesus Christ applies to these aspects of our common life.

This book is an example of how synodical government can work. It began when Dr Colin Connolly, a Reader in the Cranleigh deanery in the Guildford Diocese, brought to a discussion group in the parishes of Alfold and Loxwood the issues surrounding the theology of patenting genetic material. He then brought a motion to his deanery synod, who supported it and sent it on to the Guildford Diocesan Synod in November 2004. That Synod agreed overwhelmingly that the issues were of such significance that they should be brought to the General Synod as a Diocesan Synod Motion. So it was that on 8 February 2006 Canon John Ashe moved a motion on behalf of the Guildford Diocese calling for 'strict control on the availability of human genetic data' and questioning whether genetic material of human origin should be patented. As is the way with such motions, the original motion was amended but its central thrust was maintained. The resolution carried by General Synod asked the Mission and Public Affairs Council, in the light of the deep concerns expressed in the debate, to 'explore the theological, ethical and legal implications of patenting of the human genome' and bring a report to Synod.

At its meeting in May 2006 the Mission and Public Affairs Council decided that it wished to progress the report Synod had requested by producing a shorter book of similar length to other Synod reports such as *Sharing God's planet* and *Rethinking sentencing*. The intended readership would be the intelligent lay-Christian concerned to be informed about the issues. The publication would be designed to make readers aware of the issues so that they could contribute to the wider debate. The idea was to bring together a team of experts, Christian writers and thinkers from a range of disciplines, to examine and debate the issues. Mark Bratton, a Council member from the Coventry diocese, agreed to be team coordinator and to edit the book. So the Human Genome Review Group was drawn together and held its first meeting – to define the nature and scope of the project – on 3 November 2006. We are deeply indebted to Mark Bratton for assembling such a strong team and patiently steering their work through to the production of this stimulating book. We are also very grateful to each of the contributors for the time and effort they have put in to the exercise. This mode of working, it seems to me, is an excellent model for future handling of complex issues.

Not surprisingly, as is noted in the introductory chapter, the original production plan proved rather more ambitious than even the extended timescale allowed. Nevertheless, the product has certainly been worth waiting for. It is worth underlining that what is offered here is not a 'policy statement' from the Church of England. Rather, it is a resource for continuing debate. The essays brought together here offer the Church of England, and our ecumenical partners, stimulating and authoritative material to resource our contributions to the debates which our society needs to have, debates about the degree of regulation – legal or professional/ethical – appropriate in this complex area, the form which it should take, and why.

As has been well said, law is the 'hard edge of ethics'. That means, among other things, that rather than treating it as a 'domain of mystery', we have to engage with it, just as we have to engage with the scientific, philosophical and theological issues which are involved. Thinking across the boundaries of spheres and knowledge and expertise sounds very challenging. It is. But it is a challenge we have to undertake, both for the sake of humankind and as an outworking of our Christian discipline – 'shining the light of the gospel'. This book, and associated work which the Mission and Public Affairs Council is undertaking, is intended to help us meet that challenge, particularly those of us who are non-experts.

It is therefore our hope and expectation that the debates which follow will not be confined to those who are expert in these fields. While the issues are complex, they are of such significance for humankind that they cannot be left to experts. The explicit purpose of this book is to equip lay (in the non-ecclesiastical sense) people to engage with the issues and particularly to enable Christian people to do so. 'Engagement' is the key concept – and it means theologians, ethicists, scientists and lawyers engaging *together* to address the issues, but doing so in a way which the wider church, and the community as a whole, finds accessible.

Georges Clemenceau, prime minister of France in 1917, is often quoted as having said that war was too important to be left to generals (he actually said it was too serious to be left to soldiers, but for us the point is just as valid). That reminds us there are some matters which are so important that they cannot be left to experts, however gifted or distinguished. Dealing with the constituent parts of human life is surely one of those. So are the principles by which a community decides who 'owns' knowledge, what that ownership entails and what legal and/or ethical framework is needed to regulate its use. These are places where we need to be sure that the light of the gospel shines. I pray that this book will provide the resources and stimulus to help us, individually and corporately, to bring to bear the gospel's illumination.

Philip Giddings
Chair, Mission and Public Affairs Council
September 2008

Acknowledgements

I would like to thank Dr Philip Giddings, chair of the Mission and Public Affairs Council, for kindly agreeing to contribute a Foreword. I would like to thank members of the Human Genome Review Group for their expertise and wisdom. This group included Dr Anna Thomas-Betts, Professor Annette Cashmore, Dr Donald Bruce, the Revd Canon John Ashe, Mr John Clarke (until July 2007), Mr John Overton, the Revd Dr Malcolm Brown (from July 2007), the Revd Professor Mary Seller, Dr Michael Spence (until December 2006), Dr Peter Manley Scott and Dr Sue Chetwynd. I would also like to thank the commissioning editor at Church House Publishing, Tracey Messenger, for helping to bring this project to fruition. Finally, I would like to thank members of the Mission and Public Affairs Council for their encouragement and advice throughout.

Preface: An Anglican gene?
The lineage of this book

Malcolm Brown

The Human Genome Project is simultaneously an investigation into identity and into history. The growing understanding of the link between one's genetic make-up and who one is and how one develops raises, as we will see, enormous questions about identity and the sense of self. But our genetic make-up does not appear out of nowhere. It is inherited from our parents and their parents and so on. Our genes not only tell us a great deal about who we are but also where we have come from.

This book was commissioned by the General Synod of the Church of England through the Mission and Public Affairs Division of the Archbishops' Council, and the identity and history of these bodies go a long way to explaining the nature of the book. And, just as the genetic make-up of a person is the product of a history of human relationships, so the volume emerges from an identifiable family tree; itself the story of relationships within the churches and the theological academy and, most of all, the relationship of the Christian faith to social and political changes which continue to present the faithful with new questions, new problems and, perhaps, new consensuses.

Where, then, does this book stand in the lineage of Christian social ethics? Is it possible to locate it in relation to what has gone before, and to the wider questions of its time, so that it can be read, not just for its immediate content but as an identifiable contribution to a history of Christian engagement with pressing matters? To answer such questions, it is worth going back in time to consider how the Church has tackled this sort of thing in the relatively recent past.

The twentieth century saw the emergence of a distinctively Anglican approach to Christian social ethics, first appearing clearly between the two world wars but flowering most productively in the years immediately after the Second World War and the decades of consensual politics which followed until 1979 (a significant year for more reasons than one). In the Church, this approach is linked most strongly to the name of William Temple, successively Bishop of

Manchester, Archbishop of York and, for two short years, Archbishop of Canterbury before his early death in 1944. In the world of academic theology, it is associated with the work of Ronald Preston, whose long career brought him into contact with Temple, and with other great figures of the 1930s, such as Reinhold Niebuhr, and whose later work with the Church of England's Board for Social Responsibility, and with the World Council of Churches, made a bridge between theology as practised in the university and theology as the servant of the Church in the world. Preston was concerned that the Church's engagement with political and social issues should not only be theologically literate but should give due weight to empirical evidence and the knowledge found in disciplines other than theology – and he emphasized this for reasons that were themselves theological: a conviction that an incarnate God makes himself known to us, not only through direct revelation in Scripture and the traditions of the Church but also through our daily encounter with his created order.

Here is Preston's last published account of the approach to Christian social ethics which he had championed all his working life:

> I have thought for a long time that the best method has three stages. (1) Identify the problem. This involves a negative judgement on the *status quo*. Christians have a radical faith. They are taught not to be satisfied with things as they are and in particular to be sensitive to all who are marginalised, so they are not likely to lack issues to take up. (2) Get at the 'facts' by searching for the relevant evidence from those involved in the problem, whether as expert witnesses or as experiencing it personally. (3) Try to arrive at a broad consensus on what should be done – first of all at a middle level. This indicates a general direction at which policy should aim. Since there are always disagreements on public policies, among Christians, no less than the general public, this puts the onus on the objector if a Church Report can produce agreement on a general direction of policy. If it chooses, a Church Report can go on to recommend detailed policies, though the more detailed they are the more likely they are to be affected by the inevitable uncertainties in obtaining facts; these can often be evaluated and interpreted differently. Still more are the uncertainties in forecasting the effects of any detailed policies that are advocated.[1]

This is the classic account of what is often known as the 'Middle Axiom' approach to Christian social ethics, exemplified by Temple between the Wars and the Board for Social Responsibility between the 1960s and the 1980s.[2]

Middle Axioms emerged from a period in which the Church of England sought to maintain its role of guiding the conscience of the nation in an age of insecurity, rapid change and theological turmoil. The First World War had brought an end to the certainties – some would say complacency – of the Edwardian era, had demonstrated the grotesque inhumanity of technological warfare, and was followed by a depression which put at risk any sense of a social contract between the classes, sowing the seeds for political turmoil across Europe and the totalitarianisms which would lead to a further World War and decades of Cold War. What was the vocation of an established Church in such a world, and how might that calling be articulated publicly? On the one hand, there was the 'Christendom' movement, seeking to turn away from modernity, industrialization and urbanization and looking for inspiration in an idealized medievalism in which all human activity was ordered under God and under the benign rule of God's Church. On the other, were voices like Temple's, calling for a reappraisal of the role of faith and of theology, no longer the 'Queen of Sciences' to which all other learning was subordinate, but one significant discipline among many, which must listen with respect to the knowledge and wisdom of those whose specialisms lay elsewhere, in whose work, it was believed, God's purposes could be made manifest to the faithful. At the Conference on Christian Politics, Economics and Citizenship (1924), the Oxford Conference on Church, Community and State of 1937 and, most famously, perhaps, at the Malvern Conference of 1941, it was Temple's skill as chair and as the main author of the ensuing reports, which, if it did not fully synthesize, managed to elide the differences between these two approaches.

The Malvern Conference is worth dwelling on for a moment. In 1941 the British could feel no sense of a secure future. The Battle of Britain had postponed Hitler's invasion ambitions, but the threat had not receded significantly and the great military turning point of El Alamein had not yet taken place. Nevertheless, it was not only possible but apparently natural for a group of eminent Christian men and women to gather to address the agenda of post-war reconstruction. Malvern was convened to articulate the kind of world for which the nation was fighting and (without seriously questioning the fact of the Church of England's centrality to the nation) to paint a picture of a Church for a more just, peaceful and technologically forward-looking society.

The precise findings of Malvern do not concern us here. Like many attempts to shape the future they look, with hindsight, either bland or bizarrely over-optimistic. What is important is to recall the social environment from which commitment to the Middle Axiom approach sprang. This was a world in peril but one which held real faith in an uncertain future. It was a world which knew too well the capacity for evil inherent in the strange blend of modernism and medievalism that was Nazi fascism (although it had yet to learn the full horrors of that creed, and of totalitarian communism). In the lifetimes of most participants, powered flight had gone from being a mere fantasy to becoming what we would now call a weapon of mass destruction; a development that symbolized the advances and ambiguities of industrial modernity. In short, there were engaging parallels with our own times, but some very significant differences. The widely held dream of post-war reconstruction was one of classlessness and social (and material) equality. The autonomy and distinctiveness of the nation-state was not questioned. That dream has faded and now has little political currency. And England in 1941 could take for granted its 'Christian' nature and the central role of the Church of England as the church of all the people, an Estate of the Realm and a major part of the fabric of civilization. While the vestiges of this view persist today, few if any would regard the place of the Church as beyond question.

In the ensuing era of consensual politics, Middle Axioms became the hallmark of the work of the Church of England's Board for Social Responsibility (BSR), from which flowed a stream of reports on social issues of all kinds. The American theologian, Henry Clark, writing of the 1980s, was able to follow Paul Abrecht in describing the BSR as one of 'the two most effective ecclesiastical social action groups operating in the world today' (the other being the Roman Catholic Bishops of the USA).[3] But already the BSR stood for a tradition under question, both in the Church and in the academy. The turning point had come in 1979.

The commentator Francis Wheen marks 1979 as a pivotal year, not only in the politics of Britain but in the history of ideas.[4] As he notes, that year saw the coming to power of Margaret Thatcher in Britain and, with an even greater global impact, the advent of a fundamentalist Islamic regime in Iran under the Ayatollah Khomeini. For Wheen, both events marked a turning away from the Enlightenment values of rationality and the careful evaluation of evidence, and their replacement by conviction-, or faith-led, ideological politics. He sees the free-market economics espoused by Thatcher as another, apparently secular, version of anti-rational fundamentalism. But while there is much that is persuasive in Wheen's reassertion of the virtues of the Enlightenment, there is no doubt that Thatcher and Khomeini alike were (in their very different ways) not only agents of radical change but also symptoms of a deeper malaise that perhaps could be apprehended only vaguely or viscerally at the time.

In British politics, the consensuses forged by wartime proved fragile after decades of peace. In theology, the Middle Axiom methodology – the handmaiden, in its way, of social consensus – proved similarly unsatisfying. The charges against the BSR's characteristic approach were, retrospectively, somewhat akin to the arguments deployed by the Thatcherites against many British institutions. The method was elitist: it was, essentially, the conversation of the educated middle classes, portraying an easy, yet bogus, consensualism because the voices of conflicting interests and distinctive dissent were automatically excluded. It was, moreover, a theological betrayal, reducing the distinctive voice of the Christian tradition to a baleful appendix which added nothing to the substantive arguments.[5] In other words, a typical BSR report on an issue of social or political significance appeared to have been assembled from the opinions of experts in a relevant field (provided their views were essentially part of the liberal mainstream), reached conclusions which could have been arrived at by the leader writer of a broadsheet newspaper, and included a theological chapter which might, or might not, include significant perceptions but which had not noticeably affected the recommendations of the report. Any recommendations were likely to be characterized by a slightly defensive moderation; the voice of the Church of England as a lowly courtier daring to suggest to government that some political decisions might be capable of improvement.

If this is an exaggeration for effect, it is nonetheless recognizable to many. What is more, the criticisms of the BSR method came also from those who did not support the assault on consensus that raged through the 1980s. The contribution of the Church and of theology to public life at a time of social conflict ought, it was argued, to be capable of passion and partisanship. Cautious moderation no longer addressed the crises of the times. The difficulty was that the political right and the political left both courted the Church's endorsement and were outraged when it failed to offer it. (This angry desire to keep the Church on board political programmes may be in rather stark contrast to the relative indifference of today – two decades ago, the Churches seemed to matter to politicians more than either side was willing to acknowledge.)

Of all the Church's reports, *Faith in the City* of 1985 best epitomizes the problem and the shift of emphasis. The whole project had been conceived as a classic Middle Axiom exercise, somewhat on the lines of a Royal Commission, seeking to distil all kinds of wisdom which could address the problems of Britain's inner cities. But although the working party was made up, in time-honoured fashion, of the somewhat great and modestly good, its conception of 'expertise' extended well beyond the academy to include those whose expertise stemmed from experiencing the problems under scrutiny. Preston's last description of the Middle Axiom method, quoted above, was actually the first to include an explicit definition of 'expertise' that included the expertise of experience. Secondly, the theological chapter of *Faith in the City* took its cue, not from the pragmatic Christian realism that had characterized earlier reports but from the liberation theology tradition, then flourishing in Latin America and appearing to offer just the kind of righteous partisanship for the poor that the divisive social policies of the Thatcher regimes appeared to demand. It was this espousal of liberation theology which won for the report the epithet 'pure Marxist theology' from a Conservative minister, and thereby (unintentionally) boosted its sales and its significance.

Faith in the City was something of an exception. Many other BSR reports of the time found the achievement of consensus impossible. A short report, *Perspectives on Economics* (1984), which set out to arrive at some shared Christian thinking about the highly contentious approaches to economics adopted by the Thatcher governments, frankly admitted that positions around the table were irreconcilable and had to satisfy itself with publishing a short collection of essays on the theme of economics and faith which, taken together, were flatly contradictory. Although short, and largely forgotten, *Perspectives on Economics* was significant for its implicit acknowledgement that the BSR's classic methodology could not cope with fractious times and that the Board might be on safer ground confining itself to reports that set out a range of Christian thinking rather than coming to a (provisional) God's-eye view or at least some reasonably authoritative guidance for the Church. Liberation theology's overt partisanship was never likely to catch on in a national church which crossed party political boundaries in the way the Church of England has usually managed to.

But it was neither liberation theology nor neutrality that was to provide the most serious challenge to the classic Middle Axiom approach to public theology. The fundamental assumption that Christian theology and other disciplines could converse unproblematically no longer seemed tenable. In the BSR's reports, the theological content had felt more and more like an appendix and it seemed that the role and task of the theologian had to be reconceived if the objective of serious engagement between faith and social affairs was to be achieved. What emerged was a sharper awareness of the disjunctions between theology and other modes of thinking. If belief in God makes a difference to how people work with evidence and argument, then it is not self-evident how a meaningful dialogue can take place with other forms of knowledge and expertise where the transcendent dimension is not automatically factored in.

The status of theology as a slightly apologetic commentator on discussions happening largely outside its own boundaries was insufficient to make belief in God add up to any worthwhile difference.

One response from theology is to seek to re-establish itself as the foundational discourse which makes sense of all other knowledge. This is, to put the case with excessive brevity, the project which has emerged since 1990 as Radical Orthodoxy. Ronald Preston who, toward the end of his life, often noted history's tendency to repetition, was among the first to spot the similarities between Radical Orthodoxy and the Christendom movement of the 1930s. Both, he believed, were insufficiently alert to the necessity for theology to sit humbly before practitioners of other disciplines whose work immensely expanded our understanding of the created order without, necessarily, undermining the perspectives of faith. And it seems true that Radical Orthodoxy has not yet made a great contribution to the practical politics of lives lived in the contingent realities of the world after Pentecost and before the Parousia. Nonetheless, Radical Orthodoxy has done the Church a very great favour by re-emphasizing the profound 'otherness' of God-talk in a social context where faith has been privatized and made marginal – or even incomprehensible – to daily existence.

As has been noted by John Atherton, the mood of theological engagement with non-theological knowledge takes different turns, reflecting the contingent and ambiguous place of 'today' in salvation history.[6] Middle Axioms and the glory days of the BSR characterized what Atherton calls the Age of Incarnation – a period of history when, perhaps reflecting the largely progressive, optimistic and consensual politics of the time, it felt natural for Christians to reach for the doctrine of the Incarnation as the basis for their understanding of how world and church relate. Christ has hallowed the world by become incarnate among us, so Christians can welcome human progress as, ultimately, leading toward the kingdom, optimistic that God is working his purposes out in the realm of politics, science and human development. But, as Atherton notes, the social optimism of the post-war decades is not wholly typical of human experience, and we may be moving toward a new Age of Atonement – one in which the disjunction between heaven and earth, between the things of God and the ways of the world, are more characteristic of the way faith informs life. Here, there can be no easy accommodation with the mindsets of disciplines that have no intrinsic space for transcendence; no assumption that the solution to sin and finitude lies in the political sphere, that a touch on the rudder by good people prompted by a concerned church will keep us on track for a kingdom come on earth.

Along with the creativity of the Radical Orthodoxy movement, much thinking about Christian ethics now takes a stronger cue from the Germanic school of Karl Barth, in which the particular, indeed peculiar, nature of God's self-revelation to the world in Christ is so central. The voices of Barth and Temple or Preston had, for a long time, seemed to belong to estranged traditions.[7] Temple and Preston stood for a Church and a theology which could be modestly at ease as one of the 'Estates of the Realm' somewhere at the heart of nation and citizenship. True, Temple's classic book, *Christianity and Social Order*, had bemoaned the modern heresy that faith and politics don't mix, but his argument was precisely that this was a heresy, an aberration which those committed to the Good Society should not allow to be perpetuated. Barth's theology is for a Church which knows itself to be profoundly at odds with the culture around it. Without attempting to summarize the whole of Barth's monumental *Church Dogmatics* here, it seems self-evidently the case that the Christian faith can be assumed to be the default moral position for British people. The detachment of culture from Christianity has advanced to the point where Christian ethics is no longer the guiding hand on the tiller but one of a number of hands contesting the right to determine our cultural direction. The sense of being at odds with the prevailing culture lies at the heart of much contemporary church life, from the burgeoning of evangelicalism, to the growth of Christian lobbying groups, to the rising popularity of cathedral worship. All epitomize an increasingly countercultural understanding of faith. This is not the territory in which the Church of England's established approaches to social ethics were formed. The question then arises: does the Church of England's historic relationship with the State, and its concern for the spiritual welfare of all the people, prevent it from simply tearing up its past methods and practices of social witness, instead entering the open market of religious voices competing for public attention – or can the virtues of its tradition of engagement be harnessed afresh for a new context in which there are no precise historical parallels to inform us? More specifically, does this book concerning the Human Genome Project even begin to capture the shape and content of what such a fresh approach might consist in?

My swift canter through the history of the Church of England's public engagement with social and political affairs is intended to make clear that this work does not come out of nowhere. The Church of England has 'form' in struggling with the social ethics of such issues. Nevertheless, much within the Church, as well as in society at large, has changed since the BSR was wont to issue regular reports on such matters, and it is worth sketching in this shifting church context.

Indeed, one must start from the fact that the Board for Social Responsibility is no more, at least in its old form. It was merged in 2002 into a new Division of Mission and Public Affairs (MPA), and while the combination of the old BSR concerns with those of the erstwhile Board of Mission seemed, at first, to limit the BSR's outward-facing stance, the theological rationale is beginning to take root. The Church's engagement with the worlds of politics, science and social affairs generally now takes place in a context where the right of the Church to take a seat at the table is not only questioned but often hotly contested. Any engagement from the perspective of faith in public ethics must have a missiological quality since it cannot be taken for granted that any of the Church's interlocutors have the slightest grounding in, let alone sympathy for, the idea that ethics may look different when God is factored in. In other words, the shift in theological emphasis, characterized by Atherton as a movement from Incarnation to Atonement, and by others as a shift from cultural affirmation to cultural critique, is becoming the foundation for MPA's mode of doing theology in public. The Church's task, then, is to give expression to the distinctive ways in which believers think about ethics, and finding an authentic way to communicate this distinctiveness is subject to that most profound dilemma of all Christian mission: how to find the voice that will communicate in the vernacular of the surrounding culture that which the culture cannot easily express from its own resources. Conceiving the Church's public ethical engagements as mission immediately, then, puts the role of consensus into its proper place: not rendering consensus an irrelevance, but not making it a goal which trumps any distinctively Christian voice either.

As Nigel Biggar explains in his contribution below, the idea of Christian distinctiveness needs to be handled with some care and subtlety. The point is not that Christian opinion must be so distinctive that it cannot, by definition, be shared by others outside the company of the faithful. The point is rather that Christians should arrive at their ethical positions by an authentic process of deriving principles from Scripture and doctrine. This leaves open the possibility that others, of different faith traditions and none, may share the same ethical stance as Christians on some specific matter. It also leaves open, importantly, the possibility that Christians may disagree among themselves, since there may be more than one tenable conclusion to be drawn from the inheritance of Scripture and the Church's teaching. And so, from a very different theological starting point, one of the central features of the Middle Axiom approach is reflected within this book: the requirement for caution in formulating any final Christian ethical stance on the detailed policy implications of a specific issue, since Christians of equal fidelity and equally learned in the tradition may conscientiously disagree on the requirements of faithful living in areas where much is new and untested.

It is no secret that, on many contemporary ethical issues, Anglicans are divided. This is not necessarily a calamity. A missionary church must always struggle to discern the hand of God in the life of the world and to take the risk, from time to time, of running with social trends for the opportunities they may offer to live and preach the gospel, even though hindsight may sometimes suggest that those very social trends might better have been labelled demonic from the start. This will always be a fraught matter for faithful Christians and it is unsurprising that, sharing a commitment to mission, they will not only struggle to choose when to go with the grain of culture and when to oppose it, but will often get this wrong. Granted the scope for faithful disagreement, is a church agency like MPA reduced to publishing no more than a compendium of diverse opinions, along the lines of *Perspectives in Economics*, when confronted by a matter as complex as the human genome?

This report, patently, does not conclude with a single, definitive, Anglican judgement on the ethics of the genome project. Manifestly, the contributors have not come to a single mind. Yet there is, I think, much more here than a selection of irreconcilable positions offered to the Church, and to the reader, on a take-it-or-leave-it basis.

From the long-established Middle Axiom tradition, this book has retained the conviction that Christian social ethics cannot simply opine on subjects which involve specialisms of their own, but must listen carefully yet critically to the voices of those at work in the fields on which the Church may wish to comment. Theologically, this involves the tacit acknowledgement that other modes of knowledge than just the theological are part of any understanding of the created world. But this is not to make theology the handmaiden of other disciplines, content merely to add a Christian gloss to an analysis arrived at without recourse to theology. On the contrary, as the ensuing chapters show, theology takes up a substantial part of the work – and in far richer form than a mere commentary or appendix to the medical and scientific technicalities. Here, theology dares to question not only the pragmatic outcomes of genome research but the very understandings of the world, society and (most importantly) being human, which such research raises. This is not a work that clings lovingly to an illusory consensus but one that faces head-on the differences between a Christian and a secular anthropology.

Here, the influence of Barth and the confessional strands in Christian ethics prevent the report from working in one direction only, taking 'facts' and 'experience' as indisputable foundations on which theology must perch. On the contrary, *God, ethics and the human genome* attempts to place at the centre of Christian enquiry its theological struggle with the new questions raised by the Human Genome Project. The point is to evaluate the ways in which Christian belief moulds an understanding of what it is to be human, what might be the limits of knowledge and the place of sin in understanding the human condition. All these are germane to a moral evaluation of the Human Genome Project. To be sure, Christians are called to listen respectfully to the wisdom and expertise of others, but they do not approach the table empty handed. The theologians contributing to this book are striving to offer a set of Christian tools – or, perhaps, a Christian prism – by which new and pressing moral issues may be engaged with.

Crucial to this exercise is the necessity of wrestling with Scripture. Looking back over past BSR reports, the treatment of biblical material is often surprisingly thin. It is as if the Church of those days regarded a basic grasp of Scripture as a cultural commonplace which needed little elucidation. Now, even a glancing familiarity with the contents of the Bible cannot be assumed, and many Christians themselves – perhaps recent converts without a family history of scriptural immersion – display considerable ignorance of the wealth of scriptural material. Robert Song's chapter, here, is of great significance, not only for the fact that the Bible has been given such prominence but because Song makes the Bible simultaneously fundamental and yet problematic in the work of Christian social ethics. The fundamental role of Scripture in forming the Christian moral consciousness is clear from Song's essay. But it is problematical in that questions about the human genome are not readily resolvable through appeal to scriptural texts. We must dig deeper, striving to enter into an understanding of God, revealed in the Bible, which guides us into a Christian anthropology and teaches us how to be human in the face of new human capacities and temptations.

So, while the Bible shapes the Christian consciousness, and the Christian community – the Church – is the place where the Christian life is, however imperfectly, lived out, it remains that Christians do not live sealed off from their fellow men and women or immune to the mindsets of the prevailing culture. It seems to me that this book gives a fresh seriousness to the role of the Church and to the importance of theological resources, but it does not fall into the trap of treating Christians as the only ethically alert characters on the stage. Nigel Biggar's teasing out of the relationship between theological ethics and secular ethics is, in many ways, an Anglican tract for our time. For, more than any other denomination, the Church of England continues to understand itself to be called to minister to all the people of the nation, as well as forging and maintaining the bonds of fellowship with brothers and sisters in Christ everywhere. This Anglican vocation not only confirms the Church of England as a missionary church rather than a sect, but lays upon it the obligation to persuade and seek to influence decision makers to do the right and good thing whatever their allegiance to Christ himself.

Contrary to the assumptions which frequently inform contemporary public policy, it is now widely agreed that starting with a hypothetical 'person from nowhere' can be profoundly misleading. The ideal construct of a neutral adjudicator who has no past, belongs to no community, and lives as part of no historical narrative is not, as is often thought, the best way to discern moral principles but, resembling no one, can arrive at judgements which work only in an imagined world of ideal types. This is not a viable ethic for a Christian view of being human, in which fallible people live by imperfectly comprehended stories; stories passed on in communities which simultaneously embody God's gracious promises and are constrained by their own structural failings as mere human institutions. *God, ethics and the human genome* has tried to offer a way of approaching the world which is, at one and the same time, utterly grounded in the Christian inheritance and yet alert and open to the new depths of human understanding upon which the genome project raises the curtain.

So, how does this book fare against the critiques of the old 'BSR' approach to social ethics? Does it privilege consensus as if part of an outmoded society? Is it the elitist conversation of a particular class of commentator? Is it sufficiently alert to different perspectives and interests? Is its theology integrated or peripheral, and does it engage sufficiently with the riches of Scripture and the tradition? Does it leave room for the passions as well as the intellect when it grapples with a struggle about which people feel passionately?

And has this work abandoned or retained those things which were good and of enduring value in the established Anglican tradition of social ethics? Does it take non-theological disciplines seriously enough? Does it strike a proper balance between benign platitudes and excessively specific policy prescriptions? Most of all, does it help the Church, and its members, to come to opinions formed by faith so that their discipleship in the world can engage with the world's failings, opportunities and dilemmas?

For me, the verdict is mixed. In the book's favour, I believe that its implicit approach to consensus is congruent with the Christian understanding that, although God has made the world a place where difference and diversity are the norm, God's will is for the unity of all creation. Objective truth may be elusive in this life, but we believe (do we not?) that, under God, there is such a thing as objective truth. Postmodern relativism may be a fair description of how the world seems (some of the time, at least) but is inadequate as an ontological account of the nature of the world under God. So, in a time when ethical consensus is elusive, even between and among Christians, it is right that the work eschews premature consensus building. Some of our knowledge is just too new to come to definitive judgements. Moreover, God has not yet brought all things into fulfilment under himself, so we live with constant tensions between the persistence of sin and the reality of grace and glory – and discerning the one from the other is hard for us. Premature certainty may be a snare, and in so far as consensus suggests certainty, its pursuit may be a delusion. *God, ethics and the human genome* acknowledges difference, locates Christian theology – properly – as distinct from secular ethical thinking, but seeks to pursue a generous conversation, between people and between disciplines, which holds out the hope for a coming together, for mutual enlightenment and for shared insights, although these are not to be achieved at the cost of Christian authenticity.

Is it elitist? It is certainly dominated by a certain kind of academic voice. To that extent, the charge against the Middle Axiom approach holds good against this work also. Yet we have tried to leaven that academic tone of voice with the stories of other people, encapsulated in the case studies. True, these are themselves mediated through an academic form of discourse, but they do, I think, redeem the work from the full implications of the charge of elitism. On a topic like the human genome, there is, as yet, very little discourse that is not essentially academic (in the proper sense of that word). In time, the impact of genome research on medicine and culture may impact upon all the peoples of the world. Then a different sort of report from the Churches will be called for; perhaps one which engages with the passions – with anger, joy, delight and rage – more than this work has even attempted.

The integration of theology and other evidence has already been part of my theme. This work certainly elevates theology well beyond the status of an appendix and, given the continuing necessity to listen to voices from beyond the confessional community, the complete integration of theology in every chapter has never appeared to be a valid goal for the book. That is part of what it means to see God at work in forms of knowledge which do not, themselves, acknowledge him.

The book does not, I think, read as platitudinous, but nor does it go in for policy prescriptions, specific or otherwise. To that extent, it has more in common with such a church report as *Perspectives in Economics* rather than *Faith in the City*, in that it assembles a number of different approaches without concluding with any plan of action. But it is hard to see what any substantive recommendations might look like. Indeed, in the past, recommendations in church reports have sometimes been received in the manner of solutions, as if profound ethical difficulties could be made to go away by a few, quickly achieved, action points. Where the Church holds within itself the power to change direction – to be, as it were, a more faithful and authentic Christian community – recommendations may be in order. But the Church of England has had to learn that it rarely if ever now speaks to power in the voice of power. Where it continues to hold moral, and indeed numerical, authority, addressing the world in recommendations may sometimes carry weight, but these occasions dwindle in the face of a culture (sometimes reflected in government) which is increasingly cloth-eared about religion and the Christian inheritance of the nation. More and more, the Church's moral voice is being discovered in the conversation among its members as they explore together the meaning of discipleship interwoven with citizenship. And this is a kind of democratization process, for 'the Church' in a predominantly Christian culture is epitomized particularly in its leaders, whereas Christian distinctiveness is now a characteristic of all its members and not just those singled out by clerical dress and the grace of ordination. By eschewing the easy 'closure' of a list of recommendations, and promoting instead a careful conversation about how disciples might approach the whole genome project, I hope that this book has found the right voice for addressing an issue of this sort in the Church as it is.

On balance, then, this book does a fair job of holding together the enduring virtues of the traditional Church of England approach to social ethics with the challenges to that approach which have emerged from both the theological academy and the shifting social context in the last 30 years. Reports on this scale emerge much less frequently from the Church, nowadays: they are costly, both of time and money and have to make a calculated impact rather than be bread thrown on the waters. For all the reasons outlined above, I am convinced that this book, on a pressing, timely and intransigent moral issue, signifies a new seriousness in Christian social ethics as performed in the Church of England. It is not a final word, in terms of method or content, and time will assess its impact. But it speaks in the voice of a church which is alert to the contemporary world and to the God who is at work within it, and is simultaneously respectful (though not idolizing) of its history and the narratives which have sustained it. It is a book from, and for, a Church of England which will neither turn away from what is new nor abandon God's gifts through the centuries. And that, surely, is the Anglican 'gene' which gives us our identity and our history and which creates us anew in each generation.

1

Introduction: autonomy, solidarity and the human genome

Mark Bratton

> Be human in this most inhuman of ages; guard the image of man for it is the image of God.
>
> Thomas Merton

The purpose of this book

God, ethics and the human genome is concerned with the ethical and theological issues relating to the human genome. Although the Human Genome Working Group's initial brief involved a focus on the legal, ethical and theological aspects of the patenting of human gene sequences, it became very quickly apparent to members of the Group that the issues raised by advances in genetic technology and medicine extended well beyond the limited area of intellectual property. Within intellectual property circles, the ethical acceptability and economic soundness of gene patents were largely settled about 20 years ago.[1] However, the field of biotechnology has expanded enormously since then, catalysed in no small part by the achievements of the Human Genome Project (see below). The Human Fertilization and Embryology Bill, which as at Autumn 2008 is still working its way through the British parliamentary system, has raised a number of novel ethical issues which have emerged from developments in genetic science, technology and medicine. It therefore seemed good to the Group to tackle here some of the wider issues pertaining to the human genome as well as intellectual property issues.

The first purpose of this book is educational. It is not policy research, nor is it meant to suggest an 'official line' for the General Synod of the Church of England. Rather, it is designed to encourage and challenge readers, especially Anglican Christians, to aspire to the scientific, ethical and theological literacy required to contribute to thoughtful public debate on a topic which touches upon the very meaning of 'being human'. All the contributors are Anglican Christians, deliberately chosen as such. And although the contributors were not briefed to write from a specifically Anglican point of view, the underlying question mooted by this selection policy was whether the book, once it was published, would evince the characteristics of a distinctly Anglican moral theology, if, indeed, these characteristics exist at all.

The second purpose of the book *was* to exemplify within its pages a high-quality internal conversation between contributors, approaching the salient issues from different disciplines, intellectual formations, and ethical and theological perspectives. The contributors include scientists, lawyers, ethicists, philosophers and theologians. The idea was that the process of producing the work through meetings together and the circulation of drafts would result in individual contributions which would bear the marks of a thorough engagement with different disciplines and perspectives without necessarily prejudicing an individual's clear argumentative line. Although some of the contributions bear the marks of this form of engagement, for example Sue Chetwynd's and Peter Manley Scott's in particular, in truth, the aspiration has not wholly been realized. This is the result, not of lack of will, or ability, but of the sheer pressure of work under which most of the contributors habitually labour, and the need to bring this book to a conclusion in reasonable time.

The third and final purpose of *God, ethics and the human genome* is to draw attention to methodological issues in moral theology, in particular whether, and to what extent, moral theology should, or needs to, engage with moral philosophy. Malcom Brown, in his illuminating historical account of Christian social ethics in the Church of England, has already, very helpfully, outlined the continuities and discontinuities between the Middle Axiom tradition, exemplified in many of the publications of the now reconfigured Board of Social Responsibility, and the more overtly biblical and iterative ethics we have striven for here. Brown rightly draws attention to Nigel Biggar's important methodological contribution wherein Biggar distinguishes 'the healthy concern for the theological integrity of ethics' and a 'neurotic one for distinctiveness' (Biggar, ch. 9).There is a danger that moral theologians are wont to argue too directly from theoretical premises to practical conclusions without thinking through all the issues at ground level. There is corresponding danger, however, that ordinary thoughtful Anglicans 'in the pew' will imbibe their ethics through a media dominated by the thought of the most influential secular bioethicists, without fully understanding, let alone responding to, the demands of Christian theological integrity. As a result, the community of moral theologians, and the vast majority of Anglican Christians, end up thinking along two different circuits.

Moral theology, therefore, for the sake of its own integrity, needs to engage with the best that moral philosophy has to offer, and it is suggested that an unwillingness to do so would represent, at the very deepest level, the Church's lack of confidence in the robustness of its own premises. There can be no room for the kind of guerrilla warfare whereby the Church charges out into the public square simply in order to get its words out, before beating a hasty retreat to *fortress ecclesia*, believing, with spurious and undiminished self-confidence, that its missional obligations have been discharged in the process. By the same token, Anglican churchgoers, for the sake of their own intellectual and spiritual integrity, must be educated to bring theological concepts to bear on the challenges of living faithfully as Christians more systematically, instead of treating theology as a gloss upon, or appendix to, the default ethics that most have unreflectively absorbed from the surrounding culture.

The shape and content of this book

This book is not a seamless tapestry containing the contributions of scholars who through mutual engagement have achieved some kind of intellectual equilibrium on the subject of the human genome. The contributors represent a variety of traditions within the Anglican Church, and with a degree of mutual engagement have approached the subject from within the framework of their Anglican spiritual formation and their specialist intellectual discipline. However, there is a broad consensus that advances in human genome science raise issues of the utmost importance, with personal, social, political, as well as spiritual aspects. These contributions were enriched by the discussions that various contributors had in the context of meetings of the Human Genome Review Group, which added to the diversity of the conversations.

In the Preface, Malcolm Brown seeks to place this book in the context of Anglican moral, social and political thought, and, in so doing, provides it with a genuinely historical atmosphere. He makes it clear that the discipline of moral theology is not static and immoveable, but rather a discipline which dynamically interacts with the personal, social and political circumstances within which people live. This book takes its place within a developing tradition of Anglican moral theology which seeks authentically to speak of the living God to the contemporary world at a moment of unprecedented advance in genetic science and technology.

In Chapter 1, the Introduction, the lawyer and ethicist Mark Bratton introduces some of the book's key concepts – the human genome and patenting, in particular. He also articulates seven distinctive themes which provide an analytical framework for understanding the scientific, legal, ethical and theological aspects of the human genome. Each contribution to the book touches upon one or more of these themes from the particular disciplinary perspective of the contributor. In particular, he draws attention to the way advances in human genome science are challenging the dominance of the principle of individual autonomy in western medical ethics and law, and underscoring the importance of 'solidarity' as an ethical principle of the first order.

In Chapter 2, the geneticist Annette Cashmore introduces the reader to some of the basic facts of genetic science. She also highlights some of the main legal and ethical issues arising from human genome science with specific reference to five carefully chosen case studies concerning genetic counselling, screening, fingerprinting, therapy and research. In doing so, she makes clear that the scientific community is not cut off from, but an integral part of, society. She demonstrates, in her exposition, commentary upon and analysis of these case studies, that scientific work occurs within a moral and political context and not in isolation from the lived experience of vulnerable people who contribute to that scientific work from their own genetic resources.

In Chapter 3, the theologian Robert Song considers the biblical foundations for the traditional Christian investment in the alleviation of suffering. He is wary of regarding the genetic revolution as being in simple continuity with the Christian tradition of caring for, and curing, the sick. He stresses that Jesus' ministry of healing was unique because it pointed beyond the 'sign and wonder' of a suffering individual's psycho-physical restoration towards the promise of our final, glorious and comprehensive restoration to personal wholeness in the kingdom of God. Accordingly, Song enjoins Christians to be attentive to the dangers of an 'idolatry of cure' and the distorted and misleading understandings of the human person on which this idol is set up. Song argues that there is a close relationship between the way the human person is conceptualized and the perceived limits of responsible technological medicine. A proper biblical understanding of human embodiment, he argues, abjures the secular tendency to transcend the limits of the body either by exalting it, or denying it, in unbiblical fashion.

In Chapter 4, the ethicist and philosopher Sue Chetwynd undertakes a careful, and wide-ranging, conceptual analysis of the idea of human genome 'commodification'. She distinguishes viewing human genetic material as a 'resource' and as 'property', and, in so doing, draws attention to the blurred boundary lines between individual and collective interests in human genetic material. She argues that because all scientific research and technology is value-laden, we need to pay careful attention to the uses to which this technology is put. Chetywnd challenges us to think through, distinguish and articulate the reasons for our acceptance of certain interventions into the natural world, for example selective breeding, and our rejection of others, such as human genetic enhancements.

In Chapter 5, the theologian Peter Manley Scott argues that from a Christian point of view, developments in genetic science and technology must be judged according to 'a theological vision of the human'. Human beings are *creatures*, within whom nature and culture interact dynamically. There is therefore a good theological case against philosophies which seek to assimilate humans to, and which encourage humans to take flight from, the natural order. Scott is opposed to patents on living things because God is the source of all life. Human beings are more than merely the sum of their genetic constituents, but social and political beings. Accordingly, the scientific community cannot monopolize the discussion about the proper uses to which genetic technology might be put. Rather, as humans, we realize the 'image of God' in us by patiently responding to God's call heavenwards in interaction with the natural, social and political orders of which we are inescapably a part.

In Chapter 6, patent attorney John Overton offers a lucid introduction to patent law and procedure. He makes it clear that patents do not imply 'ownership' in the ordinary 'property' sense of that word. Rather, a patent is a contract with the state in which the state grants the patent-holder the right to exclude others from doing what is covered by the patent, in return for the disclosure of the details of the patent-holder's invention. He points out that patents are an important part of a state's commercial ecology because they encourage researchers and research organizations to undertake expensive and risky research, which might not otherwise be ventured.

In Chapter 7, scientist and ethicist Donald Bruce describes the way the commercial logic of the American and European patenting systems has controversially extended its remit beyond the human-made inanimate world to living organisms. As erstwhile director of the Church of Scotland Society, Religion and Technology Project, Bruce was substantially involved in some of the background debates and discussions that contributed to the formulation of the European Directive on Biotechnology (1998). Bruce makes it clear that public policy and law in this area is heavily value-laden, rather than ethically neutral as some advocates of a liberal patenting regime have claimed. Bruce demonstrates how the dominance of commercial interests is reflected in the way the language of the traditional patentability criteria has been stretched to breaking point. He argues that this linguistic manipulation of patent law is rationally indefensible and theologically untenable. The Christian view of the human person as an integrated totality militates against the extension of patent protection to human gene sequences without qualification or condition.

There is a distinctive mood change in Chapter 8. The theologian Michael Northcott takes a darker view of the possibilities that recent advances in human genomic science have opened up. In his view, there is a very thin dividing line between current capabilities of modern genetic technology and scenarios depicted in the film *Gattaca's* dystopic 'posthuman' vision of the future. He argues that there is already ample evidence in modern British society of a potentially deleterious symbiosis between the extension of technological control over biological processes (genetic screening, diagnosis, therapy, fingerprinting, etc.) and the desire of political authorities for greater social control (surveillance, DNA databases, etc.). This is not scaremongering, but rather an expression of Northcott's attunement to the logic of influential narratives of control which have replaced Christian narratives of 'gift' and 'destiny', and which threaten to differentiate society into castes of genetic 'haves' and 'have-nots' (e.g. in laws of insurance and employment).

Finally, in Chapter 9, Nigel Biggar offers a 'methodological interlude', in which he seeks to make a case for a robust dialogue between moral theology and moral philosophy, on which, he argues, the authority of the Christian voice in the public square depends. Biggar is clear that Christian revelation modifies in important ways what Christians perceive to be good and right, and thus provides a moral compass which orientates the Christian through the moral maze. However, he draws a distinction between the demands of theological integrity, and an often neurotic concern for Christian distinctiveness. He argues that the public square is a good deal more 'plural' than the threadbare and 'binary' distinction between 'religious' and 'secular' suggests. Christians may, by degrees, find their ethics in alignment or non-alignment with a range of non-religious ethical views (e.g. Kantians, Utilitarians and Nietzscheans, etc.). But their moral trajectory is set by biblical tradition and the Christ-event.

The shape of this introduction

This introduction is organized along the following lines. We will begin by briefly looking at the history, achievements and aspirations of the Human Genome Project, drawing attention to the patenting controversy to which the Human Genome Project gave focus. We will then consider the history of the Christian investment in the alleviation of suffering; the difficulties in defining the boundaries of medicine; and fears about the persistence in modern genetic medicine of 'eugenic' ways of thinking. We will then try to organize the various contributions around seven themes which implicitly and explicitly run throughout the book. We will end with a short reflection on what, in the context of advances in genetic science, it means to be made in the 'image of God'.

The Human Genome Project

When the US President, Bill Clinton, and the UK Prime Minister, Tony Blair, jointly announced and celebrated the imminent completion of the first draft of the human genome in June 2000, it marked nearly 100 years of progress in genetic science. The serendipitous rediscovery in 1900 by three independent research scientists of Gregor Mendel's (1822–84) seminal work on the 'traits' of the sweet pea laid the foundations for a century of scientific discovery and breakthrough. Throughout the twentieth century, convergent insights and discoveries in various fields of biology and chemistry had helped to establish the cellular, molecular and informational bases of heredity, in particular the elucidation of the structure of deoxyribonucleic acid or DNA, famously credited to Francis Crick (1916–2004) and James Watson (1928–).[2] In the second half of the twentieth century, it became increasingly clear that a greater understanding of the characteristics of human genetic information had enormous implications for the development of new, more effective, medical therapies, even if claims made for the potential deliveries of genetic science sometimes appeared over-inflated and premature.

The Human Genome Project was formally launched in the USA in 1990 and set out to 'map' and 'sequence' the human genome in order to determine the sum total of genetic information for the human species. The project began as a public sector initiative constituted by about 20 intergovernmental and transnational research groups (including the UK, China and Japan). It was widely thought that the scientific analysis of the human genome, or *genomics*, would lead to greater understanding of the molecular bases of well-known genetically related diseases such as cancer, Alzheimer's disease and cystic fibrosis. It was believed that, through greater understanding of an individual's

7

particular genetic characteristics, it would be possible to 'target' drug therapies onto an individual's specific genetic defects and metabolism, the science of *pharmacogenetics*. A greater understanding of the characteristics of genetic information would also have enormous implications for preventative medicine. If we could make informed judgements about a particular individual's susceptibility to disease, then more effective preventative strategies would become possible. In this connection, it should be noted that determining the sequence of nucleotides or base pairs in the human genome is not enough on its own to transform medicine. Scientists and clinicians will also need to interpret the meaning of this information in relation to the molecular structures and functions of the cells in our bodies before major advances in medical diagnosis and treatment can be made.

What is the human genome?

The Human Genome Project has produced information about the human DNA molecule, which is a three billion unit-long sequence of the four nucleotide bases – adenine (A), guanine (G), cytosine (C) and thymine (T) – that carry genetic information in coded form which is used by the body to build itself and function. Each base is combined with a pentose sugar and a phosphate to form a nucleotide, and linear chains of nucleotides constitute DNA. Within the nucleus of each of the approximately one hundred trillion cells in the human body, two strands of DNA are wound around each other like a spiral staircase, joined together by their complementary bases, A with T, and C with G (base pairs), and compacted and folded into chromosomes (see Figure 1). In each human cell, the total DNA (the genome) is divided into 23 chromosomes, and each body cell has 23 pairs of chromosomes, one derived from the father and one from the mother. When DNA is replicated, the complementary strands 'unzip' allowing them to be copied. The genes are particular stretches of DNA along the chromosome which code for proteins that form the body structure and carry out the biochemical processes that are essential for life. The genetic information is encoded in the bases of a gene by their arrangement in specific groups of three, called codons (TTT, or CAG, and so on). Each codon sequence codes for one amino acid, the building blocks of protein molecules. The Human Genome Project has disclosed that there are about 23,000–25,000 genes in humans, many fewer than the 100,000 previously estimated. However, these protein-coding stretches of the DNA account for around only 3 per cent of the total genome. Vast quantities of DNA therefore do not code for proteins, and have, as yet, no established role, although a small part of this non-coding DNA performs the vital function of

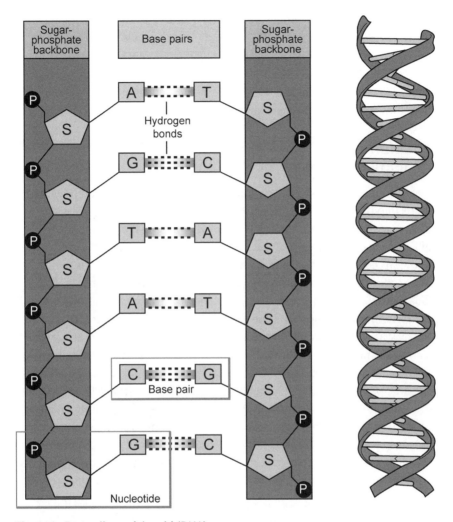

Figure 1. Deoxyribonucleic acid (DNA)

Courtesy: National Human Genome Research Institute

controlling which genes are turned on or off. Much of this apparently functionless DNA comprises particular short sequences of DNA that are repeated many times over. It is these that give individuals their personal genetic signatures and familial genetic resemblances, making possible the science of DNA 'fingerprinting' pioneered by Professor Sir Alec Jeffreys of the University of Leicester in 1984, because the actual number of repeats varies between individuals, and is inherited. The implications of this technology for the administration of criminal justice are apparent in our scientific contributor's (Annette Cashmore) final case study (case E). The term 'human genome' – it should be noted – is something of an abstraction. In reality, there are only *individual* genomes which though, of course, vastly similar, nevertheless manifest minuscule but significant differences in the order of the nucleotides. The 'human genome' of the Human Genome Project is a composite genome based on the nucleotide sequences of a selected sample of genomes drawn from diverse individuals.

The Human Genome Project and human genome patenting

The Human Genome Project was given a competitive edge when private biotechnology companies, especially J. Craig Venter who set up Celera Genomics, got involved, turning the Human Genome Project into something of a race. The involvement of the private sector raised uncomfortable ethical questions concerning the extension of intellectual property claims to human gene sequences. The adamant opposition of the Human Genome Project's idolized first director, James Watson, and the unwavering hostility of the public consortium's international partners to human genome patenting contrasted starkly with the philosophy of private enterprise. The public consortium made a firm commitment to make its information public as quickly as possible, solemnized in the so-called Bermuda Accord of 1996. This agreement bound all participants involved in the public genome effort to make all human DNA sequences over 2,000 base pairs long freely available on a gigantic online database within 24 hours of discovery. This was rather ironic given that US federal legislation (the Bayh-Dole Act) actually obliges all publicly funded researchers in the USA to secure intellectual rights on any potentially profitable discovery before releasing the information to the public.

The charismatic and entrepreneurial microbiologist, J. Craig Venter, in contrast, provoked huge controversy by filing for patent protection on gene sequences early on: 337 gene fragments in 1991 and, in the following year, 2,375 partial gene sequences. Private biotechnology companies have usually sought to recoup substantial and risky investment in biotechnology by claiming intellectual property rights. There has been a resultant commercial pressure to initiate large numbers of provisional and speculative patent applications concerning the human genome even if the relevant stretches of human genetic material being 'claimed' are currently bereft of clear functional and structural interpretation. These applications have often been drafted in extremely broad terms in the hope that further research would quickly establish the practical use of the relevant gene sequence before it was properly assessed, or that a busy or careless patent officer would overlook the broad terms in which the application was drafted. For many privately funded researchers, the prior scrutiny of research for patentability before release into the public domain is a contractual stipulation. Whether or not, in the final analysis, human genome patenting is morally right, we should recognize the transformed commercial context within which much scientific research now takes place, with many 'research-led' universities being compelled to rely more heavily on private sector funding than on government grants.

The Christian investment in the alleviation of suffering

There is little doubt that proper structural and functional interpretation of the information disclosed through human genome mapping and sequencing will lay down the basis of a major medical revolution. The unique feature of Jesus' healing ministry was that his transformative therapeutic interventions pointed beyond mere physical restoration towards that more profound and final restoration for which humanity is destined in the kingdom of God (Revelation 21.1-4). The connection between Jesus and healing and wholeness is inescapably bound up with the ecology of peace, justice and righteousness for which God has destined the world. The laudable Christian investment in the alleviation of suffering must always therefore be understood in this *eschatological* context. Jesus' therapeutic enterprise was not solely, or merely, directed to psycho-physical restoration, but rather a 'sign, instrument and foretaste' of Evil's definitive defeat, and Creation's restoration and transformation, through the life, death, resurrection and glorification of Jesus Christ, the Son of God.

While the Church was from the outset implicated in the care of the sick and suffering, the Christian theological understanding of human creaturehood, and the limits within which God has constituted us as creatures, has profoundly shaped its understanding of the therapeutic enterprise. A key element of this theological understanding of human creaturehood is the biblical conceptualization of the human person as an integrated totality of body, mind and spirit.[3] There is no biblical basis for the irreducibly *physicalist* model of the human person, associated today with certain stringent forms of materialism, manifested in forms of pride that refuse to accept the limitations of human bodily life. This form of pride is evident perhaps in the sometimes officious prosecution of ultimately fruitless technological wars against disease and illness and also perhaps in the obsession for control over the natural world which, were it possible, would find powerful purchase in the genetic enhancement of a person's evolutionary heritage.

There is also no biblical basis for the *dualist* model of the human person as an awkward aggregate of discrete body and discrete soul, which arguably encourages retreat from human solidarity and solidarity with the created order itself. We should perhaps recall the apostle Paul's stringent comments against those who tended to play down the importance of the body and morality (and therefore relationships) in favour of an idealized spiritual life (Galatians 3.1-5). This retreat is evident perhaps in the strong emphasis on an individualistic understanding of autonomy in modern western medical ethics and law, which has relegated other important cultural values to the margins.[4]

Thus, the biblical emphasis on the importance and value of the 'whole person' (Genesis 2.7) militates against a stringent physicalism that identifies the human person simply with his or her physical, including genetic, constituents. It also offers a critique of attempts to alienate a person from the natural and animal worlds of which she is inescapably a part, including a denial of the solidarity which humans, by degrees, enjoy with the rest of creation. This biblical concern with the whole person is beautifully exemplified in the gospel story about the woman with the issue of blood (Matthew 9.20-22; Mark 5.25-34; Luke 8.43-7). Jesus' transformative therapeutic intervention effected not simply her personal restoration to physical health but also a restoration to the *social* and *religious* life of her community. Within the symbolic world of first-century Judaism her physical restoration was in effect a restoration to the life of God himself. The meaning of health and wholeness is ultimately inseparable from the meaning of 'being human' in its physical, social, religious and cosmic dimensions. Accordingly, psycho-physical care and cure can only be a part of what it means to address the patient as a whole person.

Defining the 'medical boundary': disability, 'normality' and enhancement

In psycho-physical terms, advances in genetic technology have raised sharp questions about the meaning of 'healing' and the limits of the 'medical boundary'. These in turn depend largely on what we think the proper ends of medicine are. Distinguishing 'disability' from 'normality' is complicated by the messy hybrid character of the latter, which combines statistical and normative components. For example, a largely shared condition such as short-sightedness is unlikely to be construed as a disability by most people because spectacles and contact lenses are largely efficient prosthetics, even though there are lots of people around with very good unaided eyesight. Therapeutic responses to clear functional limitations, such as liver failure, are uncontroversial. But things become more problematic where elements of real harm merge into questions of social prejudice and mere human preference, for example the desire of members of the deaf community to select an embryo for hereditary deafness in order to bring the resulting child up as a fully fledged member of the deaf community. Focusing on the way many people admirably adapt to deleterious conditions, such as blindness, can obscure the actuality of loss of whole dimensions of enriching experience and thus the presence of real harm. Distinguishing *enhancement* from *therapy*, moreover, is likely to be complicated by difficulties in distinguishing genuine misery from a selfish desire to be higher up the ability scale, for example in the case of low intelligence. This is not to suggest that these various distinctions are not in the final analysis meaningful or robust, but rather to draw attention to the difficulties about defining them that need to be considered and appreciated first.

Eugenics and commerce

The eugenics movement was in the beginning motivated by the apparently beneficent desire to improve the human stock through selective breeding, whereby the genetically fit would be encouraged to procreate, while the genetically unfit would be discouraged from reproducing through financially induced sterilization or legislative coercion. This 'eugenic' mentality was pungently encapsulated by the great American judge Oliver Wendell Holmes in the legal case of *Buck v Bell* in his withering evaluation that 'three generations of imbeciles are enough'.[5] The close association between value judgements concerning the worthwhileness of people's lives and the benefits of a genetically fitter population became hideously apparent in the medical bondage and murder of the Nazi regime. Within the Christian community, and perhaps the public at large, the widespread and persistent unease with eugenic ways of thinking may relate to fears about where broader societal evaluations about certain conditions and behaviours could lead, even in non-coercive 'free-market' forms of eugenics involving selection for or against particular genetic traits. The science of 'micro-eugenics', which the Human Genome Project has made possible, involves discriminating between specific stretches of genetic code with implications for both the genetic make-up and observed physical expression of an individual.

A genuinely Christian moral theology, however it is worked out, must be of some use in helping us to discern where the boundary between the limits of medicine and the scope of the worthwhile life lies.

Seven themes

Seven themes implicitly and explicitly run throughout this book: (1) 'playing God'; (2) naturalness; (3) genetic determinism and reductionism; (4) the relationship between the human, the animal and the non-living world; (5) commodification; (6) solidarity; and (7) the relationship between medical therapies and social justice.

1. 'Playing God'

The widespread public unease that sometimes arises when major advances in scientific and medical technology are announced often induces the cry that scientists are 'playing God'. The charge seems to express an underlying unease that these advances are somehow inappropriate exercises of human freedom, born of a sense that there must be limits to the otherwise unimpeded progress of human ingenuity especially when these developments involve spectacular interventions into the natural structures of the world. Perhaps this explains the current fierce debate in the context of the Human Fertilization and Embryology Bill over the propriety of legally allowing the creation of inter-species hybrid embryos. This sense of limit may be inspired by the biblical injunctions to honour God-given limits, or it may express a broader, inchoate, perception that there are some lines that finite beings simply should not cross. The term 'playing God' is a weasel term. 'Playing God' is clearly a fundamental form of pride if we understand it to mean an arrogation by human creatures of God's status as creator. But it is wholly appropriate to 'play God' if we understand the term to refer to the exercise of that measure of creative discretion that God has given human beings in creation. 'God', as Charles Kingsley wrote in *The Water Babies*, 'makes things make themselves.'

2. Naturalness

The threadbare language about playing God is very closely related to the theme of 'naturalness', which concerns the authority God has given human creatures to intervene, manipulate and alter the natural structures of the world. A strongly non-interventionist approach is probably implausible on practical and compassionate grounds, for it would ignore the way humans have always shaped the world in ways congenial to human welfare. It would also undermine the basis of much beneficial therapy. A strongly interventionist approach, however, would raise questions about whether there are limits to human intellectual and scientific endeavour. Most would agree that humans may legitimately manipulate non-human nature to suit human purposes (e.g. the selective breeding of cattle). Therapeutic interventions into animal and human life for compassionate reasons (e.g. changing an individual's genes in a way that is beneficial to the individual himself but which will not affect his offspring) are probably acceptable to most. Whether human discretion to intervene, manipulate and alter human life includes allegedly self-serving causes (e.g. genetic screening and pre-implantation genetic diagnosis (PIGD) to produce so-called 'saviour siblings') or an organism's species-status (e.g. inter-species hybrids) are highly debatable issues.

In her philosophical contribution, Sue Chetwynd argues that the instinctively negative reaction to using genetic information and manipulating genes has not been very well thought through, even if this reaction in the final analysis turns out in some respects to be justified. Chetwynd challenges us to think more precisely about the sources of our unease with the uses to which human genetic material and genetic technology can be put. Greater clarity here will arguably help us to discriminate better between uses that are morally acceptable and those that are not (see Ch. 4). In this connection, the theologian Peter Manley Scott seeks to reconcile the tension between the 'given-ness' of nature and the demands of technological culture. He argues that the world has an 'alterable stability through time' which demands a 'patience' congenial to the welfare of the non-living and living worlds, a patience necessarily evinced in the lengthy task of selective breeding, but arguably manifestly absent in the technological surge towards genetic manipulation (Ch. 5).

3. Genetic determinism and reductionism

The strategy of discovery in the natural and biological sciences is based on the division of natural phenomena into ever-smaller constituent parts, for example organs, cell types in the organs, the interaction of proteins in the cells, the structure of the proteins themselves, and so on. This powerful practical methodology is closely associated with the ideological view that whole organisms can be primarily understood or explained away in simple and molecular terms, for example the 'selfish gene'. This methodology is also associated with a style of thinking that views the genetic composition of the human organism as the prime determinant of human behaviour – 'it's all in our genes'. The Human Genome Project is arguably intensifying these reductionist and deterministic tendencies by making possible further downward subdivision of biological reality. However, the Human Genome Project is also arguably helping to undermine this crude analysis by drawing attention to how much more the human being is than her parts. The complex combinations and interactions of genetic material, and the subtle interplay between heredity and environment, must somehow account for the elaborate totality of the human being. As Katherine Hepburn said majestically to Humphrey Bogart in *The African Queen*, 'Nature is what we were put on earth to rise above.' Theologians Michael Northcott, Peter Manley Scott and Robert Song alike draw attention to the way in which the tendency to view the human person as essentially a product of his or her genes – improvable, controllable and perfectible – can represent a refusal to accept that human beings are finite and vulnerable (see Chs 8, 5, 3 respectively).

4. The human, the animal and the non-living world

The concept of 'intellectual property' has controversially increased in scope to embrace not only the patent protection of non-living things (e.g. synthetic materials) but also living and human materials. This extension has been made easier by ongoing disputes in law and ethics about the distinction between the 'natural' and the 'artificial', on which the granting of patent protection partly turns. The participation of private corporations such as Venter's Celera Genomics in the race to sequence the human genome has raised the question of whether patent applications should be made for gene sequences for which there is no obvious industrial application. In spite of the apparently settled state of the law in Europe and the USA, the USA has extended patent protection to single-cell and multicellular organisms, such as the Harvard oncomouse, a transgenic non-human mammal (i.e. a mouse) with an artificially induced genetic predisposition towards developing cancer. The perceived qualitative differences between non-life and life suggest that the legal position will continue to be challenged repeatedly on ethical and theological grounds. The Nobel Laureate, Sir John Sulston, has forcefully argued that the distinction between 'non-life' and 'life' will become less sustainable as the gap between biology and chemistry narrows.[6] Peter Manley Scott, in contrast, argues that all life is qualitatively different from non-life and finds its source in the 'liveliest life' of all – God. On a gradualist approach, the duty of respect would not rule out the application of intellectual property rights for primitive organisms. But the more complex the organism, the greater the duty of respect owed and the greater the dangers of dehumanizing forms of commercial exploitation.

5. Commodification

The extension of the patent regime to human genetic material implies for many a change of status of that material from being part of a dignified human whole into an exchangeable commodity. It is arguably tantamount to treating such material as useful, saleable and of no value in its own right, and thus an affront to human dignity. But this sense of unease with the so-called 'commodification' of the human genome may stem more from its being treated as a form of private property rather than as a common resource for the benefit of all. The problem may not be with the application of commercial concepts to human genetic material as such, but the putative exalting of private interests over and above the collective or common good. The issues of solidarity and social justice provide a possible alternative framework within which the commercial enterprise of human genome patenting can be better understood.

Many of those opposed to human genome patenting have construed the extension of intellectual property rights to human genetic material as a claim to *ownership* of part of humanity's God-given and shared heritage. However, as patent attorney John Overton and ethicist Donald Bruce make clear in their contributions, patenting is not a form of ownership in the conventional property sense, but a commercial enterprise whereby the successful patent applicant forgoes trade secrecy in return for the benefits of legal protection of his intellectual property (see Chs 6 and 7 respectively). This form of legal protection is calibrated to balance the public interest in rewarding human inventiveness with the public interest in the dissemination of the fruits of intellectual research and the technical application of that research: 'Patenting is an ethical contract between inventor and society. Society grants the inventor protection for a limited period from anyone else marketing the invention under their own name, in exchange for publishing the full details of the invention' (Bruce, p. 88).

Nevertheless, patenting, for Donald Bruce, Michael Northcott and Peter Manley Scott, as indeed for many, reflects an unacceptable way of viewing or valuing the human genome (see Chs 7, 8, 5 respectively). The perception that the human genome is God's gift to the individual and the linchpin of humanity's fundamental unity renders the commercial exploitation of the human genome illegitimate. In the final analysis, there is, for many opponents, a vital ethical distinction between living and non-living organisms and a belief that living things have integrity that no one should destroy through forms of commercial sequestration.

6. Solidarity

The increasingly widespread recognition that persons are not isolated individuals, but naturally and irrevocably knitted into networks of relationship is encapsulated in the concept of 'solidarity'. The concept of solidarity encapsulates the importance of equality and welfare in a just society and notions of the common good and public interest. One of the startling insights gleaned from the Human Genome Project is that an individual's genetic information – putatively the most *personal* information of all – can reveal important information about the make-up of our family members and, indeed, our affiliation with the evolutionary history of life on earth. The traditional primacy of the principle of individual autonomy – which finds its legal expression in the medical context in the consent and confidentiality requirements – is arguably being subverted in the context of genetics through recognition of the incontrovertibly *common* character of genetic information. The decisions we make, for example, about our personal genetic information may have decision-making implications for family members, such as exercising the right *not to know* the potentially harmful information that genetic testing may disclose, even if this has a bearing on the actual or predictive health status of other family members. The link between our shared genetic inheritance and intergenerational relationships of dependency and mutual accountability is illustrated powerfully in Annette Cashmore's case study A dealing with genetic screening for the gene defect responsible for Huntington's disease (Ch. 2).

Moreover, the ties that bind us together are *social* as well as genetic. The separatist language of traditional concepts like 'resource', 'property' and 'privacy' are, in fact, as Sue Chetwynd makes clear, constitutively 'relational' (Ch. 4). For example, we can talk about 'shared' resources or 'collective' property, or property held on trust for another. Even the 'property a person has in himself', following Locke, does not imply unfettered rights of self-disposal, an implication reflected in well-established laws against voluntary enslavement and voluntary self-harm of an extreme nature. The sale of a car or a house occurs within a governance framework of some sort, for example you cannot leave your car to rust on the public highway with impunity. And the admixture of labour which, according to Locke, transmutes a shared resource into private property, presupposes a restriction on the monopolizing of that resource.

Most so-called private information is not, strictly speaking, 'private' because in most cases another person is usually privy to it, as Mae West well understood: 'Keep a diary and one day it will keep you.' The English law of confidentiality, for example, is perhaps best conceptualized in terms of the balancing of two 'public' interests rather than a weighing in the balance of competing private and public interests, namely, the *public* interest in having confidences preserved and the *public* interest in having those confidences disclosed in certain circumstances, for example where there is a clear and present danger of grievous physical harm to an identifiable third party.[7] Many of the human rights enshrined in the European Convention on Human Rights (ECHR), which has largely been incorporated into English domestic law, are not absolute but qualified in the public interest. For example, the right to respect for family and private life, enshrined in Article 8 of the ECHR, is qualified by a raft of public interests such as national security and public safety.

Another dimension of solidarity that the Human Genome Project has brought to recognition is the solidarity of the human species with the non-human living world through its common genetic inheritance. Annette Cashmore points out that 'We do know that more than 90 per cent of our DNA sequence is identical to that of chimpanzees, 70 per cent identical to bananas and more than 30 per cent identical to yeast, the microbial organism used in baking and brewing!' (Cashmore, p. 22).

Thus, the renewed emphasis on the reality and importance of solidarity between the human, the non-human living and non-living worlds challenges the very heavy emphasis the western legal and ethical tradition has traditionally placed on notions of personal sovereignty and 'atomistic' autonomy, the current lingua franca of modern bioethics.

7. Medical therapies and social justice

The necessarily composite nature of the human genome which the Human Genome Project sequenced has drawn attention to issues of genetic diversity, of representation and genetic discrimination between populations. The Human Genome Project is adding another dimension to the asymmetry of power which exists between the developed and developing worlds. Annette Cashmore's case studies C and D, which concern rights to the benefits of commercial exploitation of genetic material, draw attention to the indistinct borderlands of personal sovereignty and human solidarity. These highlight their implications for social justice, and further squeeze conventional notions of 'ownership' (Ch. 2). The human genome is something which, by degrees, we both share and don't share, depending on how far along the scale from the general to the particular we choose to resolve the patterns into which the human genome is organized. These case studies seem to reinforce the argument for some form of continuing acknowledgement of those who initially contribute genetic material, even if we think the concept of ownership of one's individual genome inappropriate. This continuing acknowledgement might be achieved *contractually* with groups and populations inhabiting the developed world, or, with populations in the developing world where the dangers of unfair exploitation are greater, *politically*. In both cases, there is at some level, arguably, a movement from 'commonwealth' to 'commonwealth', entailing continuing moral obligations by those who exploit genetic information towards those who supply it. Perhaps, in the final analysis, what is shared *by* all ought in some way to be shared *with* all.

Conclusion: humanity in the 'image of God'

The traditional basis for the claim that human beings are special creatures in creation has lain in the theological view that they are made in the 'image of God'. Traditionally, this view was elaborated through an emphasis on humanity's unique attributes, for example the capacity for language, reason, culture, freedom, creativity, and so on. The startling discovery through the Human Genome Project that human beings share a surprisingly large percentage of their genome with other living things (as Annette Cashmore has pointed out) has complicated the case for human distinctiveness. Yet the Human Genome Project is also making it clear that the very complexity of the human constitution cannot be crudely related to gene number, but is, more sophisticatedly, related to other factors, for example the comparatively large numbers of proteins for which human genes code and the comparatively large amount of DNA that doesn't code for protein at all. The fact that human beings are genetically constituted creatures of extraordinary complexity invites deeper reflection on the nature of the relationship between the 'whole person' and her genetically constituted parts.

The Romanian Orthodox theologian, the late Dumitru Staniloae, conceptualizes the human person as a 'little universe' (*microcosmos*) and the universe as man-writ-large (*macanthropos*). The human person paradigmatically encompasses the cosmos with an entailing vocation to 'humanize' it. The sub-personal world (within which we can include the genomic) finds its true meaning in relationship with the human person who is higher than mere nature; and the human person, by his or her very nature, aspires to find fulfilment in communion with the transcendent and free person – Jesus Christ. According to Staniloae, the rationality of the created order – even at the genomic level – is a means of interpersonal dialogue between rational human persons and the supreme rational Person – God in Jesus Christ. Any attempt to assimilate the 'whole' human person to the sub-personal, for example by reducing the human person to his genetic constituents, or any attempt to alienate the human person from his solidarity with and within the created order (including his genetic inheritance), is fundamentally *de-humanizing*, an unacceptable subversion of humanity's calling to realize the image of God within him and to humanize the universe.[8]

2

Applications of human genome information – case studies

Annette Cashmore

Introduction

The aim of this chapter is to introduce the reader to some basic genetic science and to highlight some of the complicated legal, ethical and political problems that have arisen in the context of genetic screening, therapy and research. I have presented five case studies, each containing a short scientific commentary and analysis.

The human genome project has produced information about the sequence of the three billion A, C, T and G bases in the entire complement of human DNA. This information in itself doesn't tell us where genes are, what genes code for or what genes are important in the context of different diseases. However, it provides a powerful data source from which this information can be gained following further molecular analysis.[1]

We have learnt that there are about 23,000 to 25,000 genes. These genes are the sequences of DNA that code for proteins that make up the structures of the cells and tissues of our bodies and carry out all the functions that keep us alive, and they only make up less than 2 per cent of the genome. We don't know the role of most of the rest of our DNA; much of it consists of sequences that are repeated many times. Some of these repeated sequences provide the patterns that give each of us our individual DNA identity that is used in DNA profiling and we will return to this later in the chapter. We do know that more than 90 per cent of our DNA sequence is identical to that of chimpanzees, 70 per cent identical to bananas and more than 30 per cent identical to yeast, the microbial organism used in baking and brewing! These are mind-blowing thoughts if we attempt to think about what makes us human from a reductionist point of view.

There are some genetic disorders that involve single genes, for example cystic fibrosis and Huntington's disease. Usually if a person's genetic make-up in relation to these genes is known, it can fairly confidently be predicted whether or not they will have, or develop, the disorder. Identification of many of these types of genes predated the completion of the sequencing of the human genome and used techniques of recombinant DNA technology (see Glossary at back of book) to identify and isolate an individual gene. This is a real 'needle in a haystack' problem remembering that there are about 23,000–25,000 genes and these altogether only make up about 5 per cent of our DNA! Other common disorders like heart disease, diabetes and cancer are multifactorial, involving several genes, and the identification of a growing number of these genes has been greatly facilitated by the sequence data available. However, we are not just the product of our genes; the environment also influences whether or not any genetic predisposition to a certain disorder manifests itself. For example, we may carry versions of some genes that would make us predisposed to heart disease but we can alter our environment so that we can minimize their effects. Therefore having mutant copies of that particular 'heart disease' gene does not necessarily mean that an individual will develop the disorder.[2]

The promises of the Human Genome Project were that it would provide a resource facilitating the identification of genes involved in a plethora of inherited diseases. This would lead to investigations that would enable genetic screening and also the development of treatments. Genetic screening could be of an adult, a child, or prenatal in the early stages of pregnancy or pre-implantation following *in vitro* fertilization. This information would mean that individuals could take decisions about their own lifestyle but they could also make decisions about a growing embryo or an embryo resulting from fertilization in a test tube before it is implanted into the womb. Genetic screening programmes in the population in order to determine the frequency of a particular mutant version of a gene could also be enabled. Scientific study of identified genes can potentially lead to the development of treatments of inherited disorders. There is a vision that, by understanding the variation in the genes that occurs from one person to another, it will not only be possible to develop treatments for inherited disorders but also be possible to design specific treatments for individuals. These promises undoubtedly have clear medical and social benefits.

In this chapter case studies are presented that illustrate some of the applications of the information known about DNA sequences and the human genome. This includes information gained from the Human Genome Project itself but also information that predates this. The case studies are not an exhaustive attempt to consider all of the issues but, in addition to the clear medical and social benefits arising from the Human Genome Project, they also identify issues that need wide debate. There are five case studies considered under three headings.

1.   Genetic screening

2.   Who owns our DNA?

3.   DNA databases – who owns the information in our DNA?

Each case study leaves open questions that cannot be answered by science or medicine. Subsequent chapters discuss some of the issues raised from theological, ethical and commercial perspectives and will return to the questions of what makes us human and to what extent we are a product of our genes; brave contributions to the debate!

1. Genetic screening

Many genes that are implicated in a wide range of both single gene and multi-gene disorders have now been isolated and the differences that distinguish between working copies of these genes and the versions that cause disease have been identified. This information has resulted in the development of many genetic tests that can be used to tell if an individual is carrying a disease gene, if a developing embryo within the mother's womb is carrying a disease gene or indeed if an embryo that is the product of fertilization within a test tube is carrying a disease gene. The two case studies below illustrate examples of the scenarios which could arise, and have arisen, from the availability of genetic tests. These are hypothetical scenarios but are similar to situations that have arisen many times.

Case study A

Joanne and Graham are in their twenties, were married a year ago and are now considering having children. Joanne is concerned because her grandfather (her mother's father) died at the age of 52 suffering from jerky uncontrolled movements and severe dementia suspected to be Huntington's disease. Joanne and Graham are referred to a clinical geneticist because they want to know if there is a test that would give Joanne information.

It is explained that Joanne and members of her family would have to undertake genetic counselling before a genetic test could be offered. Huntington's disease is due to a single gene mutation and it is what is called a dominant mutation.[3] We all have two copies of every gene; we receive one set of genetic information from our father and one from our mother. However, with dominant mutations just one copy being mutant is enough for the disease to show. In addition, Huntington's disease is a late onset disorder so Joanne might have the mutant gene but the symptoms of the disease would not show until later in life, typically in a person's late forties or fifties.[4] If Joanne does have a mutant copy of the gene this would mean that she had inherited it from her mother, Martha. At this time Joanne's mother does not know whether or not she has the mutant gene; she had, up until now, taken the decision not to be screened herself.

With everyone's support Joanne does eventually have the test, which unfortunately is positive for the mutant gene. The implication of this is that Joanne will develop the disease later in life and her mother will also definitely develop the disease, perhaps in five years, one year or even sooner. Given this outcome there is a 50 per cent chance that Joanne would pass on the mutant gene to any child that she might have. Joanne and Graham have decided that, this being the case, they will try to have children but will have prenatal screening to determine if their unborn child has inherited the gene and they would terminate any pregnancies for which this was the case. Joanne and Graham have successfully conceived twice but on each occasion the news was bad and Joanne had passed on the mutant gene. They continue to try.

This scenario raises several issues, for example:

- Joanne gains information about herself but also gains information about her mother.

- Joanne and her family have to come to terms with this and also with what is in store for Joanne.

- Is prenatal screening to choose an embryo that will not be affected, resulting in termination of pregnancies, 'playing God'?

There are clear social implications and family relationships would undoubtedly be affected. This family now has to deal with the incredible burden of knowing that Joanne's mother, Martha, will, without doubt, become ill with severe symptoms that will result in death probably within 15 years of their onset and that at some time in the future the same will happen to Joanne. This is in addition to the pressures of Joanne and Graham desperately wanting a child and going through the trauma of having two abortions at early stage pregnancy. One question has to be: What has been gained by Joanne having the test? There is no cure so what are the advantages? However, imagine the enormous relief and benefit to the family if the test had been negative. Other questions of course relate to the testing and subsequent abortions of the early stage embryos and decisions about abortion. What is life? Do we have the right to determine this?[5]

A possible alternative to prenatal screening involves *in vitro* fertilization followed by pre-implantation screening. This was first reported in 1990 by Robert Winston and his research team, when they screened for a DNA sequence on the Y chromosome in order to determine the sex of an embryo prior to implantation. An ever-growing number of children are now being born after such pre-implantation genetic diagnosis (PGD) for a variety of genes. The motivation for using such a procedure can be varied, including not only sex selection but also the prevention of genetic illness and generation of cells for donation to an older sibling. The case study below illustrates one such scenario.

Case study B

Mary and James have one child, Miles, who is suffering from a life-threatening blood disorder Diamond Blackfan Anaemia (DBA). A bone marrow transplant is essential for treatment but no match has been found. There is no genetic test for DBA itself but there is a genetic test that would indicate whether or not an individual would be a good bone marrow donor. Mary and James had always planned to have more than one child and they decide to investigate the possibility of going through *in vitro* fertilization, screening the resultant embryos and only implanting those that would be a match as a donor for their son. However, in the eyes of the Human Fertilization and Embryo Authority (HFEA) this was not considered to be a suitable case for PGD. A key issue was that there was no material benefit for the second child because screening was not possible to determine whether or not this child had the disease. However, the equivalent authorities in the USA would allow PGD in this case and Mary and Miles travelled to Chicago for the procedure. A second son John was born, did not have the disease and turned out to be a perfect match for Miles.

PGD of course involves *in vitro* fertilization and embryo selection. These processes themselves do raise ethical and theological debates.[6] What is the definition of life? When does life begin? Is intervention in the start of the process of life justifiable in any context? Answers to these questions are of course different when considered in a philosophical and/or theological context compared to a biomedical context. These differences are determined by needs, knowledge, goals and beliefs. Authorities such as the HFEA can give national guidelines from an ethical perspective and guidelines continually change as a result of growing knowledge, debate and also the situations experienced by individuals and society. If PGD is accepted in some circumstances, what are these circumstances? What criteria can be used to determine these circumstances? We live in a global society. Surely there must be coordination between the debates that lead to legislation worldwide.[7] Needs, knowledge and goals are parameters that can, to some extent, be quantified but beliefs cannot and, especially on a global level, it is an enormous challenge to include these in the balance of the debates.

While superficially it would seem a good idea to allow the selection of an embryo to allow the birth of a so-called saviour sibling, the case does raise issues relating to the family relationships that might ensue. In July 2004, HFEA changed the rules on 'saviour sibling' selection in response to another request to use PGD to find a tissue match for a child with Diamond Blackfan Anaemia. However, the issues relating to the case are still pertinent.[8]

2. Who owns our DNA?

Case study C

Debbie and Dan had a son, Jonathon, born in 1981. When Jonathon was only three months old Debbie and Dan noticed that he did not seem able to maintain eye contact or control his head like other babies. By the time he was six months old he was still not developing motor skills and was still unable to do things like put his fist into his mouth. The diagnosis was that Jonathon had Canavan disease. Both Debbie and Don were carriers for this recessive disorder and they had both given a mutant copy of the gene to Jonathon. Because both of his copies of the gene were mutant, Jonathon had developed the disease. This was a devastating diagnosis, because it was expected that Jonathon's brain would not develop past the infancy stage and his life expectancy was only ten years or so.

Shortly after Jonathon was born the couple set up a Canavan support group called the Canavan Foundation. Some of the work of this group involved setting up a tissue and blood bank from affected individuals and they made these available to a US doctor in order that he could carry out a search for the Canavan gene. The Foundation also gave financial support. In 1993 Dr Matalon was working at the Miami Children's Hospital and he found the Canavan gene and the mutation that led to the disease-causing version of the gene.[9] These discoveries meant that a genetic test for the disease could be developed and the Foundation made this test available cost-free. In particular, physicians were encouraged to offer the test to their Ashkenazi Jewish patients because the disorder was prevalent in these populations with an estimated approximately 1 in 60 people being carriers. Testing for carriers would potentially reduce the number of affected children because some couples would decide not to have children if they were given adequate information. However, in the meantime, unknown to the Foundation, Dr Matalon and the Miami Children's Hospital had filed for a patent on their discovery of the genetic test and when the hospital exercised its patent rights the families associated with the Foundation found themselves having to pay for the test. As they had been the people that had provided the tissue samples and the money that had made the discovery possible, they were understandably furious. In 2000 a group of parents filed a suit against the hospital; not against the patent itself but against the way in which it had been filed in secret without their knowledge.

This case highlights several important issues concerning the exploitation of research findings, as well as some issues surrounding patenting genes.[10] Clearly the patients who funded the research had rather different expectations of the outcomes from those of the researcher and his employer. Perhaps it could be said that the patients' group was a little naive. The issue of who, if anyone, owns a particular DNA sequence or sequences is also highlighted in the next case study.

Case study D

Two Canadian researchers visit the island of Tristan de Cunha in the South Atlantic because they are interested in the high incidence of hereditary asthma in the population.[11] They take blood samples from 272 of the island's 295 inhabitants, return to Canada and set up a collaboration with a biotechnology company to identify gene/s responsible and the DNA diversity that is resulting in the mutant version of the gene. If successful this work could result not only in a genetic test but potentially the development of new drugs for the treatment of asthma. These would be multibillion dollar products. However, there are no plans to share such gains with the islanders, neither in terms of financial investment nor in terms of free drugs.

This case illustrates an important issue which has been termed 'genetic piracy' and has been likened to colonialism. Here, researchers obtain samples from often remote and underdeveloped parts of the world to identify variants of genes which may then be exploited commercially or for academic research.[12] In many cases this has been likened to European explorers trading beads for much more valuable commodities in past centuries. Since the populations which provide the samples often have little if any knowledge of genetics or the uses to which the samples are to be put, they are unable to make any informed decision about taking part in the study. Some countries such as Brazil have legislated against this and now require strict adherence to codes of practice before permission is given to obtain samples. Other countries such as Iceland have viewed their genetic heritage as a natural resource and have established their own programmes to exploit it.

3. Who owns the information in our DNA?

Some of the repeated sequences in our genomes referred to above are organized in our genomes in individual patterns. The repeats are organized into clusters and the size of the many clusters and the location of the clusters among the other DNA sequences results in a unique pattern for everyone (except identical twins). All of our patterns are unique but we all get half of our pattern from our mother and half from our father. Alec Jeffreys discovered these patterns in 1984 and also realized the power that these patterns could have in individual identification. Looking at these patterns using molecular genetics techniques gives rise to DNA fingerprints ('DNA profiling' as the current techniques are more commonly known). Such approaches have affected the lives of millions of people not only in criminal investigations but in the identification of relationships, and identification of individuals following major disasters.

Case study E

Ian was driving home one evening and was pulled over by a police car. Ian thought he had been seen speeding and worried about the points on his licence. Two policemen approached Ian and asked him to leave his car and accompany them to the station. On arrival at the station Ian was asked to give a mouth swab in order that a DNA sample could be obtained and used to determine his DNA profile. During the interview it became apparent that Ian was suspected of having committed a burglary and had been picked up because his car matched that seen leaving the scene of the crime. It turned out that Ian had a watertight alibi for the offence and was never charged. However, his DNA profile remains on the database.

Some two years later Ian received a phone call from his mother with news that his younger brother, Martin, had just been arrested and charged with the rape of a young woman. The victim didn't know who had attacked her but Martin had been identified by the use of DNA profiles and was later convicted. Martin was not previously known to the police and his DNA profile was not in the database. However, Ian's was, and the DNA extracted from samples from the victim showed patterns that had half matched Ian's. So it must have been Ian's father or brother that had committed the rape.

This case study raises a number of issues.[13] The UK currently has the second largest DNA profile database, exceeded in size only by that of the USA. However, on a per capita basis the UK database is by far the largest in the world, achieved by including anybody who is arrested for a recordable offence, namely one which could, if the person were convicted, result in imprisonment. (Other countries only include convicted offenders in their databases.) This has resulted in nearly one in ten people being included on the database. About 40 per cent of young black men are on the database, and this bias could be seen as a form of discrimination.[14] Although initially approved by Parliament, the criteria for inclusion have been relaxed and it has proved almost impossible to get profiles of innocent individuals removed from the database. The legality of this retention under European human rights law is currently being challenged. The law in Scotland differs from that in England and Wales in that only profiles of those found guilty can be held on the database. Interestingly, this does not seem to significantly affect the usefulness of the database in Scotland. The use of the database to look for partial matches to identify close relatives, as highlighted in the case study, was not included in the original legislation. This gradual 'creep' of the database has clear civil liberties implications. Of course those in favour of the extension of the database will say that if you are innocent then you have nothing to fear; however, this argument assumes a benign state. It also assumes that the DNA information will only be used for the purpose for which it was collected. Although a DNA profile can only give information about identity, there are several possible developments of technology that are currently being pursued that could potentially be used for more sinister purposes. Correlating DNA information with racial origin or physical characteristics would extend the scope of the use of DNA as a forensic tool, but these developments should worry us as they could lead to serious erosion of civil liberties. It is already possible to link some specific variations in the Y chromosome to surnames, since both are transmitted through the male line. It is unlikely that this will be useful in a forensic context as only rare surnames are amenable to this type of analysis.[15] Finally, it should be noted that while the current system of DNA profiling does only give identity evidence, not only the profile but also the original DNA samples are held. From a pragmatic viewpoint this would allow re-analysis of samples should an error be found or should technology require the use of a different type of DNA profile, but it does allow the potential that further information about the whole genetic make-up of many entirely innocent people could be determined. Should we be more concerned about our genetic privacy, or can we trust the state to act in our best interests?[16]

In this chapter I have outlined some of the issues that advances in DNA technology currently raise. Genetics is possibly the fastest moving field in the biosciences, and it is hard to predict where the technology may be in even a few years' time. The ability to rapidly and simultaneously screen for thousands of mutations was viewed as science fiction just a few years ago, and yet this is now a reality. The polymerase chain reaction (PCR) now allows the rapid analysis of minute amounts of DNA and work is currently underway to further speed up the analysis. Whether we will ever see an almost instant DNA analysis is debatable but it is vital that the implications of these technologies are debated before their impact is felt on society, otherwise it may be too late to put the genetic genie back in the bottle.

3

The Bible and human genetics

Robert Song

Introduction

As with so many features of modern life, the technologies that have emerged from our new understanding of genetics seem far removed from the world of the Bible. We find it only too easy to imagine that a text whose writing was completed the best part of two millennia ago, in an age and a culture so different from our own, cannot possibly speak to our world of nanotechnology and virtual reality, of synthetic biology and transhumanist ideals. And if we are already inclined to be doubtful about the Bible's capacity to speak to us on these matters, our scepticism is only likely to be magnified when we encounter public interventions by Christians in complex technological matters which adopt simplistic or proof-texting appeals to 'the plain teaching of Scripture'. Surely, we might suppose, in these areas it would be better for us to be instructed by the best secular reasoning available, and leave the Bible to speak on the matters about which it knows?

Of course the Bible does not speak explicitly about DNA transcription or linkage studies, pre-implantation genetic diagnosis or germ cell genetic engineering. But it would be naive and complacent to imagine that we have nothing to learn from it for our own explorations of the issues raised by such developments. Even if the Bible does not share our preoccupations, we need to learn how it thinks about its own preoccupations so that our thinking can be illuminated. And doing this well involves allowing the Bible to shed its light on the underlying questions behind our own concerns.

There are many ways of framing the issues raised by the new genetics. Here I will concentrate on what is surely the central interest of the vast majority of those who research, fund and apply genetic science, namely its potential for medical benefit in the short or (more probably) long term. This medical aspiration relates most closely to what the Bible has to say about healing, for which reason most of this chapter will consider the meanings of healing in Scripture. But it is also connected to the forms of idolatry that cling closely to the desire to be cured of disease, and more widely, the desires to escape from the human condition altogether.

Healing in the Bible

Both the Church's healing ministry and its commitment to medicine rest squarely on the witness of the New Testament. They draw their intelligibility from the healing miracles of Jesus and the early Church's receiving of the charismatic gifts of healing through the Holy Spirit. Jesus' healings were clearly seen by the Gospel writers as an integral part of his ministry: Matthew reports, for example, that 'Jesus went throughout Galilee, teaching in their synagogues, and preaching the good news of the kingdom, and healing every disease and every sickness among the people' (Matthew 4.23). In turn Jesus' disciples, commissioned by Jesus to proclaim the good news to the house of Israel, were given authority to cast out unclean spirits and to heal every disease and sickness (Matthew 10.1). Later, following the giving of the Spirit at Pentecost, the apostles performed signs and wonders (Acts 2.43), including many healings: Luke gives as a paradigm example the healing at the temple gate of a man lame from birth, which turns into an occasion for Peter to speak of God's power working through faith in the name of Jesus (Acts 3.1-26). In the Pauline churches gifts of healing were listed as one of the charisms of the Spirit (1 Corinthians 12.9, cf. 28,30), and Paul himself seems to have been able to work miracles of healing (cf. Galatians 3.5), while James invites those who are sick to call for the elders of the church and have them pray over them, anointing them with oil in the name of the Lord (James 5.14-15). At many points, therefore, the New Testament makes evident the centrality of healing to both the works of Jesus and the witness of the apostolic church, and it always places its meaning in the context of the preaching of the gospel and the life of the Christian community.

It would be tempting to rest the case for the Church's embrace of medicine and medical research at this point, by appealing to a simple continuity with the healing ministry portrayed in the New Testament. And many have done so. Francis Collins, for example, the distinguished geneticist and director of the US National Human Genome Research Institute, who shared responsibility for completing the sequencing of the human genome, sees the Human Genome Project as 'a natural extension of our commitment to heal the sick'.[1] Caring for and curing those in need may be exercised through prayer and miraculous works of healing, the thought goes, but this can also be performed through the labours of doctors and nurses, of medical researchers and scientists. Both medical-scientific and miraculous approaches, we might elaborate the argument, may properly be understood as equally authentic Christian responses to the challenge of physical or mental illness. And if God has given us understanding and insight into the natural world through the gift of human creativity which science expresses, it is only right that we use that gift for the purpose of loving our neighbour in need through assiduously seeking out the causes and cures of sickness and disease.

Of course there is something that is profoundly true here, which no Christian committed to human well-being may ignore. Unquestionably there are similarities between New Testament miracles and modern western medicine. In each case the lame may walk and the blind may see. In each case the health of those in need is served. And yet perhaps we should also find something a little unsettling about this equation of miracle and medicine. After all, might it not suggest that both scientific medicine and healing miracles are different means to the same end? Might it not imply that if the doctor is unable to find a cure for my ailment, I might equally try my luck on a Christian faith healer to get what I want? Or if you find that a prayer for healing in church doesn't 'work', you might resort to a conventional doctor to meet your need, perhaps a little chastened for your apparent lack of faith? Asserting that there is a direct parallel between prayer for healing and conventional western medicine could carry the implication that there is a prior shared understanding about the nature of the problem that is being confronted, and that once our problem has been fixed we are free to return to our everyday life with our body or mind restored to (more or less) full working order but with nothing else needing to be changed.

The assumption of equivalence between medicine and healing, that they are doing the same kind of thing, runs the danger of reducing New Testament miracles of healing to paranormal irruptions of supernatural power to achieve ends that could equally be reached by the application of medical knowledge of the natural workings of the body. Indeed on this account the miracles that accompany the gospel risk being understood as no more than instances of generic 'faith healing', working through powers known or unknown to ward off threats to physical or mental health.

Yet the notion that miraculous healing is confined to physical or mental cure, or that the depth of the human problem addressed in healing is one which could be plumbed by medicine, is almost entirely abjured in the New

Testament. Two themes in the gospel narrations of healing miracles alert us to their fundamental divergence from modern understandings of medicine. The first is the frequent connection of healing with exorcism. While a certain amount of modern debate has centred on the now rather tired question of whether the phenomenon of demon possession should really be classed in terms of psychiatric disorder or recognized as something different, more interesting is the relation of deliverance from unclean spirits to miracles of healing. At times the two seem to be clearly distinct: Jesus' disciples 'cast out many demons, and anointed with oil many who were sick and healed them' (Mark 6.13), which seems to imply that exorcism and anointing with oil were addressed to different afflictions. In Luke, on the other hand, we find the two languages converging: Jesus 'rebukes' a fever as he rebukes an unclean spirit (4.39,35), and declares a woman free who had been bent over for 18 years by a 'spirit of infirmity' (see Luke 13.11-12). Yet, whether they are to be distinguished or not, both healings and exorcisms together accompany the good news of the kingdom that Jesus proclaims (Matthew 4.23-4, Mark 1.38-42). Both represent deliverance from the powers that oppress human beings, whether those powers be understood as organic physical or psychological disorders, or are personified and individualized as demons. The connection of healing with exorcism suggests that healing is not just a matter of medical cure, but also represents a defeat of the powers of evil.

Second, the Gospels make clear that healing miracles have a meaning which goes beyond mere psycho-physical cure. The association of healing with deliverance from demonic powers is the special case of a more general truth about their connection with Jesus' preaching of the kingdom of God: the healings by Jesus and his disciples both point to, and are themselves part of the substance of, the coming messianic age. In response to the bewildered charge by critics that his power to cast out demons must be the result of his being in league with Beelzebul, Jesus retorts by proclaiming that his power is the power of God's kingdom: 'if it is by the Spirit of God that I cast out demons, then the kingdom of God has come to you' (Matthew 12.28). That demons recognize who Jesus is and realize that he has come to destroy them are signs that the kingdom is near and that the overthrow of the powers of evil is imminent (Mark 1.14-15,23-7). And this defeat of the forces of evil is inseparable from a wider vision of God's new age in which healing forms an integral part. This broader panorama is perhaps most clearly indicated in the programmatic manifesto set out in Luke 4: here the anointing of the Spirit of the Lord to bring good news to the poor is linked to release for captives, recovery of sight for the blind, freedom for the oppressed, all in a Jubilee year of God's favour which Jesus declares is now present (Luke 4.18-19,21). Jesus' healings are themselves part of the substance of the new era: to experience healing is just to participate in the reality of the eschatological age. But they also form one seamless part of a broader pattern of liberation that is psycho-physical, social, political, and indeed cosmic, in nature.

These New Testament emphases develop and focus themes which are only fully intelligible when understood against their Old Testament background. One example of this is the language of 'signs and wonders'. This is used recurrently in Acts (5.12, 6.8, etc.) to describe the miracles that accompany the spread of the gospel, but it is the same language as is used in the Old Testament to refer to God's saving actions in delivering Israel from Egypt (Exodus 7.3, Deuteronomy 4.34, Jeremiah 2.30, etc., reflected in Stephen's speech before the high priest and council (Acts 7.36)). Indeed for the Old Testament the primary context in which the vocabulary of healing is used is not so much the individual patient as the nation. It is in the context of the inconstant responses to God by Israel as a people that the correlations are developed that characterize Old Testament thinking between relationship with God and well-being – between sin and sickness on the one hand, and repentance and healing on the other. As they have turned away from God as a people, so they are judged and experience suffering as a result; when they repent of their waywardness, so God turns to them in forgiveness and they receive healing. 'Come, let us return to the Lord,' declares Hosea, 'for it is he who has torn, and he will heal us; he has struck down, and he will bind us up' (6.1). Similarly, according to the Chronicler, following the dedication of the Temple the Lord makes a promise to Solomon that 'if my people who are called by my name humble themselves, pray, seek my face, and turn from their wicked ways, then I will hear from heaven, and will forgive their sin and heal their land' (2 Chronicles 7.14). The scope of this healing and restoration is not only for human society; by extension, it is seen as cosmic and all-embracing. Thus in Ezekiel, it can come to include ecological renewal of the natural world (Ezekiel 47.8-12).

But if the primary context of the language of healing is national, this does not of course exclude prayer for recovery for the individual who is suffering. The Psalms are notable in this regard: 'Be gracious to me, O Lord, for I am languishing; O Lord, heal me, for my bones are shaking in terror' (Psalm 6.2). Often, it is not entirely clear whether the Psalmist is suffering from the guilt of sin or the pain of illness (cf. Psalm 41.4, 103.3, etc.), which only serves to emphasize the connection between the dimensions of forgiveness and healing in salvation. Yet the relations between individual and national suffering, and

between physical illness and disobedience, are affirmed and brought to
a culmination in God's promise to the people after the deliverance from
Egypt, that

> 'If you will listen carefully to the voice of the LORD your God, and do
> what is right in his sight, and give heed to his commandments and keep
> all his statutes, I will not bring upon you any of the diseases that I
> brought upon the Egyptians; for I am the LORD who heals you.'
>
> (Exodus 15.26)

Healing and salvation are finally in the hands of God.

We may infer from these Old Testament emphases that when Jesus preaches
the good news of the kingdom with signs following, those signs are to be set
against an entirely different background of intelligibility from our own medical
and scientific search for physical and psychological cures. The healings that
mark the kingdom point towards and participate in the final eschatological
fulfilment of creation. As an integral part of a salvation which is not only
personal, but also social, political and ecological in nature, they show that
psycho-physical wholeness is connected to the context of the restoration of
right relationships and the establishment of justice. Conjoined with the defeat
of the powers of evil, they indicate the cosmic overcoming of the order of sin
and death that was achieved on the cross. Attending the preaching of the
Church born at Pentecost, they confirm that the Spirit that raised Jesus from
the dead is at work in this world.

The idolatry of cure

As a corollary of this, the New Testament writers also display an abiding
concern that miracles of healing not be misunderstood. Because the desire to
gain relief from suffering can be engrossing, and can absorb all the energy,
love and money that one is capable of mustering, healing can come to be
sought as a final goal without any view to any wider goods or greater
meaning. Signs and wonders can be desired for their own sake, not for the sake
of the Christ to whom they point.

This theme is found in the Gospel of Mark. The early chapters show Jesus as a
worker of healings and miracles: indeed Mark devotes the greatest proportion
of all the evangelists to these. Jesus is described as having mastery over disease,
for example in his healing a man with a leprous skin disease (Mark 1.40-45), a
woman suffering chronic haemorrhaging (5.25-34), and a man with severe
speech and hearing impediments (7.32-7). And he is also depicted as having

mastery over nature: he quietens a gale on Lake Galilee (4.35-41) and twice miraculously modifies bread and fish so that the hunger of huge crowds can be satisfied (6.31-44, 8.1-21). But Jesus is also importunate that his disciples see beyond these: 'Do you still not perceive or understand? Are your hearts hardened?' (8.17). The turning point of Mark's Gospel comes with Peter's recognition in Caesarea Philippi of Jesus as the Messiah, the immediate result of which is that he teaches that he must suffer and die, and that his followers must expect to suffer as well (8.27-38). To see Jesus only as a wonder-worker and not as the suffering Messiah is to misinterpret him entirely, and is part of the reason for his stinging rebuke of Peter that his mind is focused 'not on divine things but on human things' (8.33).[2] Miracles and healings do accompany the preaching of the kingdom, but to be absorbed in them alone is to miss the plot of which they are part (cf. John 6.26).

Indeed seeking signs and wonders, and the power that comes with them, for their own sake, can be positively dangerous. We see this in the story of Simon the magician, whose own proficiency in magic had astonished the people of Samaria. Recognizing the superior power of the Spirit, he is baptized; but his obsession with power remains, and he offers money to the disciples in the hope that he can dispense the power of the Holy Spirit himself – a request which receives the crushing response from Peter: 'May your silver perish with you, because you thought you could obtain God's gift with money!' (Acts 8.20).

The constant danger that power is used not to point to our dependence on Christ, but as a way of evading Christ and the demands of the kingdom, can finally be unveiled as a form of idolatry. In Paul's account of it, this is a matter of worshipping and serving the creature rather than the creator, and as a breach of the second commandment of the Decalogue, is never far from a breach of the first, holding other gods before God and exchanging the truth of God for a lie (Romans 1.25, cf. Exodus 20.3-6). The dangers of idolatry inevitably increase the closer they get to the things that concern us most, and the avoidance of sickness and the death it portends are at the summit of these. The self-deception in which we engage, and the belief that we are pursuing what is good and wise, is equally likely to escalate in such circumstances: Paul talks of human beings who with darkened thinking claim to be wise, but who in fact have become fools (Romans 1.21-2).

Perhaps the greatest form of idolatry is the refusal to remain a creature. The primordial sin is precisely acting with the intention of being 'like God', as the serpent insinuates may be possible (Genesis 3.5). To refuse one's creaturely status is implicitly to deny that everything which God made is good

(Genesis 1.31): it suggests that a better deal is to be had elsewhere. But, while the Fall has corrupted the creation, human vulnerability to the contingencies of life is not a kind of mistake. Rather it is the intrinsic form in which human beings are constituted as creatures, that is as those who are incapable of sustaining themselves, but are continuously upheld by the mercy of God in whom they live and move and have their being. Sickness therefore has a dual role. On the one hand, as a result of human fallenness it is a standing reminder of the alienation of human beings from their original created goodness: to experience suffering is to encounter the existential reality of human fallenness. On the other, under providence it can also act as a means of glimpsing the insight that human beings are not self-dependent but can only ever find the source of their fulfilment from beyond themselves. They do not have to labour under the burden of being the source of the meaning of their existence, to toil anxiously to maintain or stretch the number of their days, or to struggle under what Karl Barth calls 'the intolerable destiny of having to give sense, duration and completeness' to their lives.[3] Human vulnerability, rather than being the cause of a simmering sense of resentment which from time to time flares up into an enraged hatred of human powerlessness against an implacable universe, can be the source of a profound recognition of being sustained by God. 'My grace is sufficient for you, for my power is made perfect in weakness', learns the apostle as he groans under the burden of an unidentified thorn in the flesh (see 2 Corinthians 12.7-10); and his lesson about being upheld by the power of Christ is paradigmatic for Christian experience.

Science and medicine in a secular world

Does all this mean that there can be no role for medicine, since healing is always God's work? Or that using technological science in the cause of medical research is an idolatrous attempt to seize powers that will lead us away from Christ? Assuredly not. For the Church, it means that prayer for healing is always set within a broader eschatological context, and is inseparable from the story of the final salvation of humanity and indeed the whole cosmos to which it points. Healing therefore will always involve faith: 'your faith has made you whole,' Jesus says to the woman who suffered chronic bleeding, 'go in peace, and be healed of your disease' (Mark 5.34). But it can never be merely 'faith healing' or the quasi-magical manipulation of known or unknown forces; indeed it may have been precisely to avoid any implication that healing might be a power at the disposal of particular individuals that Paul refers not to 'wonder-workers' or 'healers', but to 'deeds of power' and 'gifts of healing' (cf. 1 Corinthians 12.28). And because both faith and healing are finally gifts of the living God, healing is not something which is the causally necessary response to a self-induced feeling of psychological certainty – a state of mind which might superficially seem like faith but is in truth an effort at healing by psychological works, as becomes clear when people attribute their lack of healing to their not having believed sufficiently strongly.

Moreover, because healings are signs of the kingdom, Christians can never be resigned to sickness. Within the context of the dependence on God that prayer signifies, care for one's health through appropriate diet, hygiene and exercise are part of Christian faithfulness. Similarly the use of medicine and medical and scientific knowledge is entirely proper: Christians may not indulge in a refusal to use human understanding of the natural workings of the body on the grounds that this is somehow morally inferior or spiritually less faith-filled. Christians delight to share the wisdom of Ecclesiasticus, in a celebratory passage on medicine that is lengthier than anything to be found in the books regarded as canonical by Jews and Protestants:

> Honour physicians for their services,
>> for the Lord created them;
> for their gift of healing comes from the Most High,
>> and they are rewarded by the king.
> The skill of physicians makes them distinguished,
>> and in the presence of the great they are admired.
> The Lord created medicines out of the earth,
>> and the sensible will not despise them . . .
> And he gave skill to human beings
>> that he might be glorified in his marvellous works.
> By them the physician heals and takes away pain;
>> the pharmacist makes a mixture from them.
> God's works will never be finished;
>> and from him health spreads over all the earth.
>
> (Ecclesiasticus 38.1-4,6-8)

Health is from God, and by God's grace doctors minister healing and take away pain, while pharmacists (perhaps this is the nearest reference the Bible has to medical or genetic research) use their God-given skills to manufacture medicines out of the natural world that God created.

This understanding of science and medicine also bears on the practice of medicine in a secular context, where God is not explicitly recognized as the source of all being. Even if the world does not acknowledge or praise its creator, secular science and medicine, together with the cultural understandings and expectations with which they are bound up, may obliquely witness to God's goodness and God's rejection of all that distorts the creation. Even if medicine cannot of itself restore a person's relationship to God, it can at least recognize that healthcare addresses the individual as a whole, not just the physical body in isolation from the integrated psychosomatic person. Even if it cannot bring about eschatological *shalom*, it can at least recognize the social and environmental dimensions of human well-being. Even if it cannot justify people before God, it can at least acknowledge that there may be intimate connections between people's health outcomes and the justice and equity of the social structures within which they live.

There is therefore in principle a role for technological medicine, including genetic medicine, which is part of creaturely activity and uses God-given skills, whether or not they are recognized as such, for human health and well-being. It can form part of a pattern of expectation of healthcare which appreciates its limitations and does not imagine that it can solve all our problems or form an alternative means of salvation. Medical treatment can be offered in a way which helps us to live with our frailty, rather than pretends that we need never suffer. New genetic techniques can be used in service of the health of the body, not as a means of escape from the body. The power which they confer on those who wield them can be used for the good of patients, not as a means of self-aggrandizement. It is fully open for such techniques to be used in a way which bears its own indirect witness to God and does not distort the story of human creatureliness.

Ethics and enhancement

The application of this to the particulars of the new genetics is a matter of detailed and extensive discernment, some of which is the subject of the following chapters in this book. No doubt most everyday clinical practice by geneticists and genetics counsellors harbours no illusions about the salvific possibilities of medicine. In a time when the gap between diagnosis and cure frequently remains unbearably wide, outstandingly more pressing is some elementary alleviation of the suffering caused by genetic disorders and some immediate respite for the shattered lives they can leave in their wake. Any incremental advance in our understanding of genetic disease is something to be celebrated.

Yet not all applications of new genetic knowledge may be quite so straightforward. While much research aims at the deployment of more powerful techniques to fight medicine's traditional enemies, there has also been wide speculation about much more expansive appropriation of these powers. Conjectures about enhancing evolution and removing the body's natural imperfections, whether by improving physical or mental capacities or by extending life, have bred feverish hopes in certain quarters for a posthuman future in which beautiful, strong and intelligent people will have sloughed off the frailties of the body as currently constituted. Visions like this may be far from ordinary clinical experience, but they are not the less important for that. They inhabit our cultural imagination and reflect some of the deepest aspirations of the modern world. And in a technological society reality is the child of the imagination.

Instinctively we sense that this desire to enhance the body aims at something rather different from the therapeutic desire to ward off disease, and a variety of languages have been employed to mark the contrast: 'therapy' versus 'enhancement', 'corrective' versus 'non-corrective' interventions, to name but two. Yet despite this quite deep-seated intuition, it has not proved so easy in practice to articulate the underlying distinction between them. Besides, sceptics have asked, even if the distinction can be made, what precisely is supposed to be wrong with enhancement? For example, if we are entitled to improve our child's life-chances through education, why may we not achieve the same goal through genetic manipulation? Indeed, if we have a moral obligation to educate our children as best we can, would we not also have a moral obligation to use genetic enhancements to improve their underlying capacities if these were available and safe to use? Theologically, might we not even see these improvements as prefiguring the resurrection life, especially if they can make us less violent, more sociable, more capable of empathy?

One common way of addressing this has been to appeal to the image of God. Whether by exploring the Genesis passage (1.27) in its literary and historical context, or by reading it in the light of Christ as the image of the invisible God, the one in whom God's original intention for humanity takes form (Colossians 1.15), the thought has been that we might be able to deduce from the idea of the image of God some criteria for normative humanity. Yet this has not proved very successful: after all, it is unclear what aspects of Jesus' humanity should be regarded as normative for humanity in general, and what should be seen as contingent features of a particular first-century Palestinian male. Similarly inconclusive has been the effort to distinguish those interventions which merely restore disorders that are the consequence of human sinfulness from those which actively enhance particular traits; this simply raises the question of how we could tell which disorders result from human sinfulness.

It is arguable that Scripture does not have much to say about what are normative human physical characteristics. But this does not mean it has nothing to say. Instead of trying to discern physical norms for the body from Scripture, it may be better to consider the story Scripture tells about the body. For the New Testament does know of a decisively modified body, with a genetic and physical constitution which is continuous with but somehow startlingly different from our current bodies. The resurrection body, unlike our perishable bodies, will be imperishable (1 Corinthians 15.35ff.), yet this will be the result not of human technological manipulation, but of the work of God. Inquiry into the exact nature of this body is met by Paul with a single withering word: 'Fool!' (1 Corinthians 15.36).

However, even if we do not know the constitution of the transformed body, we do know the kinds of actions which are appropriate to those who will inherit the kingdom of God. Many of these are explored in different parts of 1 Corinthians, as Paul considers what it means for Christians to be part of the Church, that is, part of Christ's own body. For example, because of their primary identification with Christ, Christians must eschew any behaviour which is likely to exacerbate the social or economic advantage of some Christians over others. Paul constantly exhorts the rich and powerful among the Corinthian Christians to make way for the weak, whether it is in relation to eating meat sacrificed to idols (ch. 8) or to equitable sharing in the Lord's Supper (11.17-34). Any application of new genetic technologies which might lead to the intensifying of current power differences must therefore be questioned. Similarly dubious are any attitudes or practices which imply that the body is indefinitely malleable and manipulable to suit the desires of the self, or that the body can be separated from and opposed to the self: among those Paul opposed at Corinth were those self-proclaimed 'wise' who believed that in their gospel freedom it was a matter of indifference what they did with their bodies (6.12-20). Christians will also find themselves opposed to any practices which signify that human beings are finally self-dependent and not reliant on God for their sustenance. 'Flesh and blood cannot inherit the kingdom of God' (15.50), and it is precisely because Christians believe in the resurrection that they will be wary of any mentality that fosters the denial of human finitude and mortality through anxious efforts to render this perishing flesh invulnerable to death.

Instead of finding in the Bible a set of normative criteria for appropriate forms of intervention in the body, we are given ways of helping us understand what is involved in genetic manipulation. The questions the Bible puts to us are not immediately applicable to genetic engineering in any crude way; rather what is put in question are deeper questions about the aspirations of modern western culture as a whole. Would our use of these new technologies inequitably enhance the power of the already powerful? Would they imply a subtle kind of rejection of our bodies as the source of bad in our lives, rather than helping us to embrace our bodiliness as in some way the good – if fallen – creation of a loving creator God? Would they engender the perhaps unspoken assumption that we can be the ground of our own being, and need no longer look to God for our creation and preservation? Questions like these require very delicate handling and careful discernment, and will not yield ready answers. But it is only if we are prepared to ask them that we will be able to sift through what in new genetic technologies will ultimately enslave us, and what will ultimately liberate us.

Conclusion

I have not attempted to address the biblical context of all the issues that are raised by developments in the new genetics. For example, I have not touched on questions of property that are raised by gene patenting, or of confidentiality, or of the multitude of particular moral issues that are so numerous that some have even proposed a new field of 'genethics'. Perhaps most importantly, I have left aside questions about how we are to think of human embryos, which are crucial to thinking through many core technological developments in reproductive genetics.[4] But in thinking through what the Bible has to say about healing, about the idolatry that surrounds our desire for cure for its own sake, and about the desires that lead us to want to transcend our bodiliness altogether, we may find our own thinking profoundly touched. Even if the Bible does not always share our questions, we need to let our questions be questioned by its questions; and in letting our answers be answered by its answers, we may in the event find ourselves transformed and healed as well.

4

The human genome and philosophical issues

Sue Chetwynd

Introduction

As we have seen from the case studies in Chapter 2, there are many ethical issues that arise in consideration of how we deal with our genetic heritage. In this chapter we are going to concentrate on three particular areas. The first, which is illustrated by case B, is the issue of commodification; whether any exploration of genes and genetics necessarily leads to regarding living things, and perhaps humanity in particular, as something useful, saleable, of no value in its own right. That is, is the second child in case B just regarded as a source of bone marrow for his brother, rather than a person in his own right? Secondly, we will think about whether there is anything inherently wrong in using the knowledge we acquire in our investigation of genetics. Some may think we just shouldn't be investigating or manipulating genes; that this is in some sense 'playing God'. And finally we will consider whether specific areas of genetic technology lead to ethical problems. Again this will consider issues that arise in our case studies; whether information about someone's genetic make-up is their private property, or belongs partly to others (case A); how genetic material obtained from someone can be used and whether they are entitled to any profit from those uses (cases C and D).

Commodity and resources

So firstly we will consider the issue of commodification, with its assumption that to think of human beings and parts of human beings as commodities is ethically wrong. There is a worry that the Human Genome Project by its very nature involves commodification of what is human. We need to think about why we feel commodification of the human is wrong and whether investigating and using genetic information does essentially or necessarily involve commodification. So what do we mean by commodification?

A commodity is something essentially for sale, something with a commercial value. In fact we could say that its value is created by the marketplace. A commodity is worth what someone will pay or exchange for it. And this may be one of the things that we dislike about thinking of humans and their bodies as commodities – that they are given a market value when we feel they shouldn't be. However, we should also beware of talking of the market as if it were something impersonal, which has nothing to do with us. A marketplace is made up of human beings; it is we who are doing the valuing, and doing it in terms of commercial value, thinking of the sorts of things which can be bought and sold. Furthermore, the same thing may be a commodity to one person and have a different value to others. For example, when a local authority wishes to serve a compulsory purchase order on a house, they view it only as a commodity and offer a price based on its market value. The person whose house it is may value it more for the memories and importance it has in their own life. So we may think of commodification as viewing an object as something to be sold, with the implication that perhaps it shouldn't be, or that its value is different from (perhaps greater than) the one it might have in a marketplace.

It may be useful to compare the concept of commodity to that of resource. A resource is something we can make use of, but is not necessarily for sale. We can understand the difference here in the use of the term 'Human Resources' for what used to be personnel departments. A resource has a value relative to what it can be used for. It may also have a value independent of its use value. For example, a horse may be useful to a farmer in terms of the farm machinery it can haul around, but be valuable as an animal he loves and cares for in its own right, so that even when it is no longer useful, he may still care for it. The fact that something is a resource does not, however, mean that it has to be a commodity. The farmer may sell his horse when it is of no more use, but he does not have to.

However, seeing something as a resource means seeing it as some 'thing' we can use, and this may lie behind some of the unease we feel when thinking of human beings and parts of their bodies in this way. The important difference here between people, or any living thing, and other resources, may be to do with whether it is acceptable to regard them only as a resource, or even, given they can be of use, whether they should be used in this way. This is rather similar to an idea used by the philosopher Immanuel Kant. For him human beings have moral importance because they are able to think for themselves and make their own decisions. Because of this it is important for Kant that we should not use other people purely to further our own interests. His Categorical Imperative says: 'Act in such a way that you treat humanity, whether in your own person or in the person of any other, always at the same time as an end and never simply as a means.'[1] However, we should note that he doesn't deny that we do and can treat other people as means, just that we shouldn't only treat them as means. In our terms that means that regarding people and parts of their bodies as a resource would not be wrong, provided we don't regard them solely as a resource, but as people in their own right, with their own interests and importance.

We have already seen that, in some instances, we regard human beings as resources – they are useful to employers, for example. However, we are less happy about regarding them as commodities; employees are not seen as something to be sold. In the case of body parts we may have slightly different feelings. We tend to regard body parts as a resource; that is, in the western world at least, we think it is acceptable, with consent, to use parts of our bodies, such as blood or organs, for the benefit of others, particularly if the resource is replenishable, such as blood or bone marrow. Some religious groups are unhappy about giving away either organs or blood, for example Jehovah's Witnesses, or some Orthodox Jews and Muslims. However, even if donating organs and tissue is acceptable, there is not universal agreement about the selling of human body parts. In some parts of the world it is certainly acceptable to sell blood to a blood bank, and it is even acceptable to sell organs. So some, perhaps most, see it as acceptable to regard human beings and parts of them as resources, but not to regard people as commodities, though we are less sure about organs or blood.

Perhaps what matters here is not what we actually do in various parts of the world, but what implications that has for how we value human beings and their bodies. As Christians we may regard God's valuation of human beings as paramount, and understand how we should value one another in the light of that. Again this is a theological issue and will be dealt with in later chapters. However, we can still consider whether regarding people and parts of their bodies as either resource or commodity values them in some unacceptable way.

We have seen that regarding something as a commodity or a resource values it as something saleable or useful. However, this may not be the only, or even the principal, way of valuing it. We do see other people's organs as useful for transplantation purposes, but this does not mean that we value people only as a collection of useful spare parts, or only as a good employee, even though they are valuable to their employer. In case B, the parents wanted another child; they just also wanted one who could help Miles. So even if we recognize people and parts of their bodies as resources, something that can be used to help others, we can do this while, as Kant would insist, still valuing them as who they are. In fact people who receive blood or organs from others typically do regard their donors as more than a resource, as people who have, because of their own concerns and values, helped them. If we want to say that people should not be regarded at all as a resource, then we will have to condemn blood, marrow and organ donation, not just using genetic resources.

When it comes to thinking of commodities the valuation seems to be a more important issue. Although, as we have seen, something can have both a commercial value and a personal value, perhaps the feeling about people and their bodies is that they ought not to have this commercial value at all, that they ought not to be the sorts of things we think of as commodities. What sorts of things shouldn't be sold, or what is the right way to value things? If we regard something as saleable, then we must also see it as being someone's to sell, that is, as property. It may be that the reasons we are unhappy regarding something as a commodity are to do with whether we think it can or should be regarded as property.

Property

What allows something to be regarded as property, or what might mean it couldn't be property? And does it make a difference whose property we are considering it as? Is it common property, collective property, private property, property held in trust or not property at all? We might start by considering John Locke's views. In his *Second Treatise* he says, 'Though the earth, and all creatures, be common to all men, yet every man has a property in his own person: this nobody has any right to but himself.'[2] So he thinks of all nature as the common property of humanity and for its use, and of people as having a 'property in their own person'. It is not clear quite what having a property in your own person could mean. It could mean that we possess our bodies or are able to control them, or it could mean we have the right to decide what to do with our own person. Property, particularly private property, is to do with issues of access and control, who has a right to do what with particular resources. Locke goes on to argue that people acquire things 'common to all men' as their own private property by mixing their labour with them and thus making them their own. However, he does think it is important that this process still leaves enough of the common resource for others. So, for example, the farmer can capture a wild horse and train it to be useful for him. He has mixed his labour with what he got from nature, and has therefore made it his property. But Locke would think it wrong of him to capture and train all wild horses, even supposing this was possible, so that no one else could use or own any horses.

So Locke thinks of the resources of the earth and its creatures as common property, the property of humankind, some part of which can be converted to private property by someone's mixing their labour with it; and of human beings as their own property. We should also be aware of a collective notion of property, where the use of property is determined by the community for the common good. This may be concerned with how a country uses its tax income, for example, or what planning regulations to have, which restrict what I may do with my private property in pursuit of the common good. Another way of thinking of ourselves and our bodies, which probably fits better with a Christian view, is not as something that is our own property outright, but more like property held in trust for another.

Locke's view seems to fit fairly well with our existing feelings about human beings and their bodies. If we are our own property, then no one else can sell us, although this doesn't actually rule out our selling ourselves. Similarly if our bodies belong to us then we can give or sell parts of them to others on this account. Even if we think that blood or organs should not be for sale, we still seem to regard them as the property of donors, in the sense that they have a right to donate them. Interestingly, the situation may be different for cadaveric donation of organs. At the moment in this country, we regard it as someone's right to donate their organs after death (although this can be overridden by relatives), but any system such as an opt-out system (where you would have to register that you did not want your organs to be used, rather than saying when you did) seems to regard body parts as closer to common or collective property. On the other hand, if we regard our bodies as gifts from God, to be used and disposed of according to his interests, then we need to be able to discover on an individual or collective level how God would want us to use our bodies, and therefore also our genetic material, which this book may be attempting in part.

Of course most of our cases are not concerned with donating genetic material to others, although that may be a future possibility, but with discovering or altering our genetic nature. We should therefore be thinking not so much about how we use our bodily resources, but how or whether we can 'customize' the body we have been given. Are we rejecting God's gift if we try to change our genetic nature; are we trying to improve on God's work? These issues will be discussed in more detail in later chapters, but again we need to think about how making genetic changes differs from other changes to our bodies that we, as a society, allow people to make, from dyeing our hair, or tattooing our body to cosmetic or corrective surgery.

Genetic material as property

So we may, in different circumstances, think of ourselves and our bodies as held in trust from God, or our own private property, or sometimes a collective resource. What problems might this raise for us when we come to think about genetic material in particular?

There are two areas of concern here: the human genome, that is human genetic material in general; and the individual genome, the genetic material that is an individual's, my genome as opposed to yours. The human genome looks like something we might regard as a natural resource, and as either common or collective property. Since knowledge about the genome, and what can be developed from that knowledge, can be used to benefit us, we seem to see it as something that should be used to benefit us all, not something reserved for the private benefit of a person or company. Some of our unease about patenting seems to be concerned with whether what should be a common or collective resource can be privately owned. Here we should bear two things in mind. The first is that, as John Overton explains in Chapter 6, patents are not really about ownership understood as possession; they are about returns on investment or reward for labour. In this they incorporate something of Locke's concept of mixing your labour with something. The second issue is about what it is that is patented. We talk about patenting the human genome, and that sounds as if it is directly going against what Locke says, as if someone is annexing for their own private profit what ought to be available to all. But is that really what is happening? Let's think about some resource like oil. It would be wrong on Locke's account for some oil baron to acquire all the oil in the world. But it wouldn't be wrong to acquire some oil, develop a means of processing it into a useful product, and patent both the process and the end product. The end product is not, after all, the oil as it comes out of the ground; it is a development of that. If this is what is going on in gene patents, if what is patented is a genetic test developed from knowledge gained from study of the genome, it may not seem so problematic. Of course there may be other problems about how we ought to be able to use genetic material, but we'll come back to that later.

So we have one issue about whether the human genetic heritage is a resource that should be available to all, and not be possessed by anyone for their own exclusive use and benefit. However, another problem is that we are all sources of genetic material – do we individually have rights in our genetic material, is that our private property? If my genetic material has been donated for research use, and it has been developed into something that is patentable and making money, should I benefit from that? This is the sort of question that arises in cases C and D. Let's compare this again to the case of the oilman. If he has already paid me for the right to extract the oil, I don't seem to have a right to further recompense because his labours have made him a fortune – although I may charge him more in future to extract more oil. But there are two differences here. Firstly the individual has often, indeed mostly, not been paid for use of their genetic material. They perhaps agreed to its use in a spirit of altruism to benefit humanity in general, to add to the span of human knowledge. And unlike the landowner who granted oil extraction rights to the oilman, there may be no need at all for the researcher to get more genetic material if they can replicate what they already have.

Much may depend here on how the original material was obtained. Was it a gift given altruistically to further medical knowledge? Did the donor agree to its being used for a specific purpose, or for general research? Were they aware that its use may lead to profit for the researchers? Does it make a significant difference that what is developed could only have come from this particular group of donors – is it a scarce resource? In Annette Cashmore's case C, the problem is that what was freely given to help other members of a community now seems to be denied to both them and the original donor, except at a cost. Much may depend, however, on the nature of the relationship between the Canavan Foundation, the researcher and the Miami hospital. Was it clear that the Foundation intended the information and benefits to be freely available, and had they agreed this with the researcher and the hospital? The important issues here seem to be to do with consent, and the appropriate reward for input. It is an important principle of research ethics that, if people donate material for research, they consent to its use, sometimes in specific terms and sometimes in general terms. If such consent has been obtained without coercion, with the donor having a reasonable understanding of the research and its potential outcomes, and the use of the material is in accord with the consent, it is not clear why it would be wrong to make a profit from it. The alternative would be to say that it is wrong in general to profit from research into the human genome, or any research which uses human tissue, in which case, of course, no one will do any such research. But if material is obtained without consent or without the donor understanding what it may be used for, then its use at all is morally problematic, regardless of profit issues. As to whether the donor should share in the profit, the researchers may argue that they are the ones who took the risks and costs of developing the end product – it may have produced no results after all. If so, they are the ones who, in Locke's account, have mixed their labour with a natural resource, and are therefore entitled to the rewards of their labour.

Ownership of genetic information

There is another area in which we might think of issues of privacy, if not entirely of property, and that is to do with genetic information. We tend to think of information about us as our private property, at least in the sense that we are entitled to control who acquires that information. Although some information about all of us is in the public domain, we have strong feelings about private information, and our right to control who should have access to it. The question is whether genetic information is like this. Information about the make-up of my own genome looks like it is my private information, and therefore I should be able to control who knows it. However, my genes are not, in some sense, mine alone. I share some of them with the entire human race, and a lot more of them with my close family. The problem arises when I have some information about myself which may impact on others, and whether they have a right to that information as well. Certainly there are circumstances where we think that is the case. If I have a notifiable disease and am a danger to others, the local health authority has a right to know this. If I am claiming benefit and my circumstances change, the benefit authority has a right to know. There has been a lot of debate recently about whether parents of young children have a right to know about those convicted of sex crimes living in their neighbourhood. People who are the result of fertilization by donated eggs or sperm, or those who are adopted, claim a right to know who their parents are. So there are many areas of life where either the risk to others, or the misuse of public funds, or even strong feelings of identity are accepted as reasons for knowing what might otherwise be regarded as private information.

This question arises with respect to genetic information because screening may discover information about an individual which has implications for other people's health or welfare. In case A we saw that Joanne's discovery that she is a carrier of the Huntington's gene also reveals that her mother must be. Suppose Joanne's mother does not want to know this, since Huntington's is incurable. Does this mean Joanne should not have the test? If she has it, it will probably be impossible to keep the result from Joanne's mother. If I have a genetic tendency to breast cancer, does my life or health insurance company have a right to know? If we were ever to discover a genetic tendency to undesirable behaviour, should others be entitled to know that I may be violent or aggressive? If we decided that there was a right to know information about others, there might also be a question about whether others could insist that we were screened for various genetic characteristics against our wishes. Many of these are issues that, as a society, we have either not considered, or are unsure about, but we need to think about the sorts of possibilities our knowledge of genetics and the uses we might make of it raise.

So far then, it looks as if, unless we feel genetic material is different in some special way from other human body parts or products, we should not have particular problems in thinking of it as a resource. In that sense it seems that the Human Genome Project could be regarded as not essentially commodifying genes, although it may be exploring their nature, perhaps with the intention of discovering their uses as a resource. As research this seems to be little different from many sorts of medical and biological research into the nature and workings of the human body, or any living thing. The problems come when we think of whether genetic material or information is rightly regarded as property. And if so whether what we are concerned with is private property, which is how we might regard our own genetic material, or common or collective property, which might be how we regard the human genome, with genetic information sometimes being seen as one and sometimes the other. Seeing the human genome as a resource may encourage us to think of it as the property of the human race, common to all men, as Locke might think of it. This way of thinking of it will tend to make us wary of how individuals might use it, and whether that use will be detrimental to the rest of us. But we also tend to think in terms of our individual genetic material and information, and whether we have rights to control how that is used, or the sorts of changes we might be able to make to ourselves by manipulating genes. None of this means that use of genetic material, whether individual or common, turns it into a commodity, or means that its only value is as a marketable resource, although neither does it rule this out. So the important issues we seem to be left with are to do with how such material could be used, who may benefit from its use and in what ways.

The ethical use of genetic materials

In this section we will first of all consider whether technology as such is something that is neither right nor wrong but value-neutral. If, as we will see, it is not, then we have to ask how we might evaluate genetic technology, and in particular we will consider four uses of genetic technology to suit humanity's purposes: changing non-human nature, changing ourselves as individuals, changing or selecting the genetic nature of others, and changing the nature of humanity.

What is the moral status of technology? We've suggested that the Human Genome Project is about discovering the nature of the human genome, and as such is to do with obtaining knowledge. Manipulating genes is, however, a species of technology. It could be argued that obtaining knowledge is neither right nor wrong; it is how we use that knowledge that leads to moral issues. However, as we'll see in later chapters, even obtaining knowledge says something about the priorities of our society which can be criticized. Some have argued that technology is value-neutral in the same way; processes and tools or mechanisms are neither good nor bad it is how we use them that introduces moral issues. The difference with technology, however, is that when we make things for our use, the sorts of uses we expect to put them to are part of our understanding of them. So we incorporate purposes into our artefacts and processes. This means that they cannot be value-neutral in the same way as perhaps the discovery of knowledge can. So, for example, we might claim that the technology that is intended to cure or minimize suffering is good, the sort of technology that is intended to harm is bad, and that much of technology falls between these two extremes. Medical technology on this account generally has a positive value; weapons technology would perhaps have a negative value, but much technology could be used for good or ill; the car may be rushing someone to hospital, or allowing the bank robbers to escape more easily.

The moral status of genetic technology

When we come to looking at genetic technology then, we have the possibilities that it is either generally beneficial, generally harmful, or that it is a mix of beneficial and harmful. The purposes of genetic technology are to manipulate genes – to eradicate them, introduce them, replace them or modify them. Is such manipulation always for beneficial purposes? Certainly our case studies show that, even if the initial purposes are beneficial, there may be harmful consequences; the possibility of information about one person telling another something they didn't want to know, the possibility of a person being regarded or treated just as a resource for someone else's benefit. And some of the possibilities discussed in later chapters, such as discrimination based on genetic heritage, don't look very beneficial. So it looks as if we cannot say that genetic technology is unequivocally beneficial.

Is it generally harmful, and why might we think this? Well, given that our intentions may be largely beneficial, it would be generally harmful only if there were something wrong about the very idea of manipulating genes. There are at least two possibilities here: the idea that in manipulating genes we are 'playing God', and the idea that this is interfering in the natural order in some unacceptable way. If 'playing God' means somehow usurping God's role in creation, we would have to show how genetic technology does this in a way that other, particularly medical, interventions do not. For example, most people would see nothing wrong in assisting conception, although that might be seen as usurping God's creative role. A similar point can be made about interfering in the natural order. The practice of medicine in general is interfering in the natural order, or at least interfering with natural processes. Disease is natural, so working to prevent or cure it is interfering in a natural process. We would need to say what might be special, therefore, about genetic technology that might make this sort of, otherwise acceptable, interference unacceptable.

Perhaps interfering in the natural order is to do with whether we think that genetic change changes what something is, changes its place in the natural order, in a way that other modifications we can make do not. No one would think I become a different person because I have my hair cut, or even because I have cosmetic surgery. If I receive a transplanted organ from another person, I am still the same person. Similar points might be made about genetic changes to plants and animals. Selective breeding, for example, makes changes to plants and animals, but does not change what they are in any essential way. But genetic manipulation allows us to move genes from one species to another, in ways that selective breeding cannot achieve, so perhaps this is the source of our unease. This unease about genetic change may depend on the idea of genetic reductionism mentioned, which will be discussed in the theology chapter as well as here. This is the idea that what a living thing is depends entirely on its genetic nature. In this case we would decide whether something was human, not because it looked human (a store mannequin?), or behaved in a human manner (a sophisticated robot?), but because it had the right genetic make-up. Along with this might go the idea that the only important thing about human beings is their genetic make-up, and that everything about them could, in the end, be explained in terms of this. If something's essential nature depends on what its genetic make-up is, and particularly if there is a feeling that we are changing its God-given nature, then changing that make-up may change what it is. We will come back to this discussion when we talk about blurring the boundaries.

A further problem is that perhaps we do not know enough about the complexity of the genetic environment and that we therefore risk doing more harm than good. This would be analogous to difficulties we have had in the past with ecological problems. When plants or animals have been removed from or introduced to the environment, there have sometimes been unforeseen undesirable consequences. In the same way, introducing, removing or changing genes may have unforeseen effects in the genetic environment. Although some genes may be linked in very simple ways to particular effects, it is likely that many are interlinked in complex ways. However, even if there is a very real possibility of making mistakes, this is not necessarily an argument for doing nothing in this area. It does mean we should be cautious about what we do and take the risk of harm seriously. However, many medical procedures have been extremely risky in the early stages, and we have still persevered with them.

So far then, we have considered whether genetic manipulation is essentially beneficial, whether it is 'playing God' or interfering in the natural order, whether it makes essential changes to the nature of things in a way that other interventions do not, and whether it is too complex for us to understand and therefore to proceed safely. In the first case we have seen that, although its aims may be beneficial, some of its effects may not be. In the second we would need to make a case for why genetic manipulation causes moral problems that other, already acceptable, interventions do not. And in the third case that while, as with all new technologies, we may through insufficient knowledge do more harm than good, this would not be an argument that genetic technology is essentially morally problematic, but a good reason for being cautious about what we do until we have a fuller understanding. The issue about whether it makes essential changes to the nature of things in a new and morally worrying way, we will discuss later on. But unless that, in and of itself, makes genetic technology morally wrong, then the moral problems may lie in the particular ways we use such technologies.

The problems of using genetic technology

There are four areas of use of genetic technologies that we consider, each of which produces its own problems, and all are to do with changing nature to suit our own purposes. Genetic technologies may allow us to make changes to the non-human natural world (plants and animals), to ourselves as individuals, to other human beings as individuals, and to humanity in general. So let's think about these in turn.

Changing non-human nature to suit our purposes

Although there are many moral considerations to do with our use and manipulation of nature for our own purposes, the use of genetic technologies does not raise many special problems. Throughout human history we have thought it acceptable to use natural resources, living and non-living, in ways that suit us. We have modified living things to suit our needs, breeding plants and animals to be more productive both in terms of amounts produced and in terms of type of product, and seen nothing wrong in it. So again the problem here hangs on whether manipulating genes introduces a particular type of wrong. It surely cannot be that we are making potentially irreversible changes, since selective breeding may also do that. In fact genetic technologies may allow us to restore species and types that may have been thought to be irretrievably lost to us. It could also be argued that selective breeding, which we regard as acceptable, is indirect genetic manipulation, so why would it be wrong to directly manipulate genes, perhaps producing the effects we want more efficiently? Some may be uneasy with the speed of such change compared to selective breeding. This could be a worry about speeding ahead in ignorance of the consequences, which again is an argument for being careful, but not for stopping such advance altogether. Or it could be a worry about disrupting the stability of the natural or God-given order – introducing so many changes that there are no clear categories of creation any more. This is far beyond our abilities at the present, but it seems to be part of the worries we will consider in the section on blurring the boundaries.

Changing ourselves as individuals

There are two sorts of ways we can envisage using genetic technologies to change ourselves. One, somatic changes, involves making changes to an individual's genes, in a way that will not affect their descendants. This would be, for example, correcting my genes to eradicate my cystic fibrosis, but not stopping me from passing it on to my children. The other, germ-line changes, would allow the latter, that is, changes to the genetic make-up of my reproductive cells to allow change to be passed down the generations. Some of our unease may centre on finding it acceptable for individuals to choose what happens to them, but not for them to make choices for others, particularly if the choices are risky ones.

An embodiment of this idea can be found in John Stuart Mill's Harm Principle.[3] This is essentially a political principle and says that it is only acceptable to interfere with other people's liberty to prevent them from harming someone else. In fact this distinction between what we can do to ourselves and what we can do to others is quite important for Mill. He argues that, as long as we are mature adults, and understand what we are doing, we can risk, or even do, harm to ourselves, and society should not interfere. The reason is, he says, that we generally know what will be best for our own happiness. However, it is the duty of society to protect others from any harm we may do to them, and this applies particularly to those who are not in a position to make competent decisions for themselves. So deciding to have genetic change made that will only affect me is acceptable, but to make those decisions for others, particularly if there is potential for harm, is not.

Christians, however, may also have concerns about how acceptable it is to modify even ourselves, if we see this as attempting to improve on God's handiwork. This will be discussed in Chapter 5 on theological issues, but we should still bear in mind that we do change God's handiwork in other fields of medical treatment without necessarily condemning it. Something like this notion of hubris may be the basis of a distinction we make between what we might call change that is corrective (removing my cystic fibrosis) and change that is non-corrective (improving my looks or intelligence). At the moment we can do none of these things, but perhaps we should be thinking of them now, rather than reacting to them when we can. Non-corrective change could perhaps include things like changing genetic structure to increase lung function for enhanced sporting ability, or perhaps some of what we now do by cosmetic surgery could be done by genetic change. Again, however, we must bear in mind that this may not be a problem particular to genetic technology. What we think it acceptable to do by way of cosmetic surgery, or medical techniques in general, raises the same or similar questions. If it is acceptable to give growth hormone to someone who, without it, would attain an adult height of four feet (correction), is it still all right to give it to someone who would be of average height, but aspires to be a basketball player and would like to be over six feet (enhancement)? We may approve of facial surgery for someone whose face has been ravaged by disease or accident (correction), but worry about doing so for someone who just does not like the way they look (enhancement). Although similar problems arise with genetic manipulation, it does not seem that they are specific to this technology, as they are not something especially problematic for this way of changing human beings.

Mill would think both sorts of change equally acceptable, provided the individual concerned understood the risks and advantages, but as a society we have a tendency to protect individuals from harming themselves under some circumstances, though not under others. So we might have to consider what changes we would regard as acceptable, and what as harmful, but as was said above, this is not a decision only applicable to genetic technology.

Changing other people to suit our purposes

When it comes to making changes that affect others, however, the Harm Principle comes into effect. This appears to reflect the uncertainties we might have about making changes to our germ plasm, that is, changes to us that will affect our descendants. The same sorts of concerns may also surround the ways we might use genetic technologies to effect changes to others, particularly our offspring. Too much use of terms like 'designer babies' tends to obscure the issue, so let's think of the sorts of situations we could be considering.

Firstly there are the issues of genetic screening and pre-implantation genetic diagnosis (PGD). Here the genetic make-up of embryos is considered, and ones with undesirable characteristics are rejected or not implanted. Actually this is not changing anyone's characteristics, it is choosing one embryo over another on the basis of its genetic make-up. Now admittedly this involves rejecting some embryos that have already been created, but again this is not peculiar to genetic technology; we already accept procedures like assisted conception, which involve not all embryos created being implanted. We may have different attitudes to this, but someone who accepts *in vitro* fertilization (IVF) as a technique to aid infertility would have to show what is different about embryo selection on the basis of particular characteristics that makes this unacceptable. Again, of course, we might make the distinction made above, between eradicating defects, and selecting for enhancements. We might think it acceptable to reject the embryo with congenital deafness, but not acceptable to choose the one which will be female, more intelligent, or tissue-matched to help a sibling. In justification of this, our first response might be to say that we should avoid causing harm to the child we choose to bring into being. That, of course, would not, at first sight, argue against choosing in favour of being female, more intelligent or of the helpful tissue match. However, it may bring to mind the problem we discussed at the beginning of this chapter. Is choosing characteristics for a child turning them into a commodity?

This question also arises with respect to our second possibility, that of specifying in advance the genetic make-up of our offspring. We cannot do this at the moment, but as it may be possible in the future, we should consider the possible impact. As was said above the issue arises here also of choosing freedom from defects or health problems, as opposed to particular preferred characteristics such as fair hair, blue eyes, a specific gender, high intelligence or sporting ability. Is this commodification of our children? Well it doesn't seem to be to do with selling them. The concern here is more about whether we consider them only as objects, repositories of certain desired characteristics, rather than as people in their own right. Are we thinking of them in the same way as we might think of our next car? With the car, we don't find this morally problematic because it has no interests of its own, and no value other than the one we give it because of its characteristics. People, however, have their own interests in how they live their lives, what they make of them, and are valuable in their own right, independent of the characteristics they have. The worry is that, if I design my child to have certain characteristics, my expectations will mould her life, and leave her no room to make her own choices. Perhaps children may feel under pressure to measure up to the expectations of their 'genetic design'. Will a child designed to be intelligent, if this were possible, feel more of a failure if they aren't, than a child who isn't so designed, but whose parents place a high value on intelligence? These are real issues, but they are surely issues about parenting rather than specifically about genetic manipulation. We tend to condemn those who try to mould their children into a path that those children haven't chosen, however they try to do it. We all come into life with certain characteristics and certain potentials. As long as we are permitted, like anyone else, to choose how to live our lives and what to pursue, then it is not clear what harm has been done by having fair hair, or any other characteristic chosen for us.

A further problem may be whether we select embryos not to avoid an undesirable condition, nor to enhance their abilities or characteristics, but to have a characteristic that most of us would regard as undesirable. There was a case recently where a deaf couple wanted to choose a congenitally deaf embryo for implantation, on the grounds that the resultant child would fit in better with their community and way of life.[4] Now perhaps most of us find it hard to envisage wanting to choose to have an impaired child, although we may also be unhappy with aborting such a child. However, Mill's Harm Principle doesn't help us here. If we were to choose a deaf embryo we would not be harming it; the choices for that embryo are an impaired life or no life at all. So it is not so clear why it would be wrong to do this. If IVF hadn't been used, this deaf child may have been born anyway. Is leaving things to chance morally better than choosing, or just another way of choosing? This may be a worry about playing God again, which will be discussed in the theology chapter (ch. 5), but it leads us in to our third level of intervention.

Changing humanity to suit our purposes

There is a further concern with changing people, since one thing we may be concerned about in selecting certain characteristics is that we may change not just individual people but humanity irretrievably. These concerns range from worries about reducing the gene pool, to blurring the boundaries between species, to creating something that may be no longer human, or may be superhuman.

Changing the gene pool

The first concern is either a development of our worry about our ignorance of the complexity of the genome, about not knowing what we may be losing in making changes, or that if we all select for fair hair and blue eyes, then red hair and green eyes may die out. The former we have already noticed is not specific to genetic manipulation, and although a reason for caution, is not necessarily a reason not to explore this area. The latter has two strands to it. The first is about whether the changes are serious or trivial. If the genes we risk losing are, or may be, really important to humanity, we should beware of losing them. If they are not, then it is hard to see why this may cause a moral problem. Admittedly it may not be possible to say which genes will be important, and therefore it may be wise to keep a rich gene pool. But that brings in our second strand, which is to do with whether this risk is real. This argument assumes that everyone will go for the same sorts of characteristics. Red hair will only die out if everyone prefers fair hair. There seems a fair amount of evidence, however, that people don't all value the same characteristics in their children, and if this is true then there may be no risk to the gene pool. Even if we did all opt for the same characteristics, random mutation would mean that the gene pool would not stagnate. Many of the conditions that are genetically based arise not because we inherit them from our parents, but because of changes in our genes that happen due to outside effects, or to miscopying of genes in the reproductive process. So, for example, 80 per cent of cases of achondroplasia (a variety of dwarfism) are due to new mutations rather than inherited characteristics. It seems unlikely, therefore, that choices made about the characteristics of our children will drastically change the gene pool of the human race.

Blurring the boundaries

Blurring the boundaries between species is something we first thought about when considering possible changes to plants and animals, but it also arises with respect to people. If we can shift genes from one species to another, we may be doing something of a quite different order from selective breeding. If we do this, will we disturb the natural order of living things? Might we change things so much that the boundaries between plants, animals and humans, or between different species of plants and animals, are no longer maintained?

The question depends on an assumption that there are natural boundaries. So we might ask firstly, are there such boundaries, and secondly, if there are, does introducing genes from other species breach those boundaries? In one sense it seems quite obvious that there are boundaries – a zebra is quite different from a kangaroo, an oak tree from a pansy, and a human being from a whale. But how different is a horse from a donkey or a zebra, or a wolf from a dog? So what distinguishes one species from another? Biologists certainly used to distinguish species one from another on the basis of whether interbreeding would produce fertile offspring. If that is the case, then introducing new genes would only be a problem if it prevented interbreeding that already existed, or allowed interbreeding that didn't already exist. However, it may be that species are now determined on the basis of their genetic make-up. Here we have more of a problem. We can perhaps say at this moment that the chimpanzee genome differs from the human one in certain specific ways, but it hasn't always been so. Scientists now think that humans and chimpanzees had a common ancestor as recently as 5 million years, or 30,000 generations, ago. We are told we share 90 per cent of our genome with chimpanzees, and even a fairly high percentage with bananas. So it may be that relatively few genes distinguish species from one another, and over time this both has changed and may continue to do so. So it may be difficult to say what counts as the boundaries of a species, and how they may be breached.

Species – genetic reductionism

Let's think about this in terms of human beings for now, while remembering that similar points apply to other species of living things. The arguments above assume that what it means to be human, or any particular species, is given by our genetic make-up. It reduces humanity to the, possibly rather small, subset of our genes that are different from other species around us. From the point of view of biology this may be adequate. We may want to insist, however, that what is important about being human, or anything else, is not reducible to the biologist's viewpoint, or entirely given by our genetic make-up. Admittedly that contributes a large amount to what we are, but if that were all there is to it, in the individual case at least, we would have to say that identical twins were the same person. So at least at the level of being individually who we are, we want to claim that there is more to it than genetics. If this is so, it is not clear how changing our genetic make-up would risk losing or changing our humanity. Being human is surely at least as much about the ways we live, order our society, treat one another, and the sorts of relationships, commitments and responsibilities we enter into as it is about our biological make-up. While genetics may have some effect on these things, it is surely not the only thing that does so. Later chapters will discuss the idea that to be human is to be made in the image of God. But however we understand that, it surely does not mean having a specific set of genes, any more than it means having the particular bodily shape we have.

Inhuman or superhuman?

If what we are worried about is changing human nature so drastically that it can no longer be recognized as human, we might want to consider who will do the recognizing, and what counts as being human. Different societies have at different times recognized varying categories of people as human. In our fairly recent past we have had societies who have claimed that some races were not really human (Jews, or non-whites), and even in this country we have only fairly recently begun to treat women and children as people in their own right, with their own interests, rather than the property of some man. Most people nowadays would agree that we have to show some relevant difference to account for treating people differently. Even societies that do treat parts of their society differently from the rest feel the need to justify their behaviour. If this is so, then even if changes were made to people to make them look very different, or to have very different characteristics from the ones we have now, we would still have to justify why those differences should be grounds for treatment as non-human. It may be that we could change over time radically enough for groups of us not to be able to interbreed with others, in which case we may have different species of humans, but that is surely not to say that we have to regard some of them as human and some not. If our humanity is not just about our genetic make-up, then these differences may not be relevant anyhow.

The discussion so far has been about how or whether human beings recognize one another as such. The important thing from a Christian point of view is surely who God recognizes as human. Although again this will be discussed in later chapters, it seems a special form of hubris to suggest that we can change humanity so much that God can no longer recognize us.

Conclusion

None of the above is to say that there are no worries about genetic technologies and how they might be used. We may not have the knowledge to proceed safely, we should think about the harm we could cause to others by manipulating our or their genes, and we may need to consider how we regard and treat people who are changed by genetic technologies. All this is an argument for thinking about what is important about being human, what we may be able to do using genetic technologies, and the good and bad effects this may have. But it is not necessarily a reason for condemning all work with genetics out of hand, nor classifying it as necessarily leading to regarding people solely as collections of genes that may be useful and desirable or their opposites. Investigating the nature of creation as it appears in our genetic make-up does not mean that our genes, or we, have to be seen purely as a resource or a commodity, although what we discover could be very useful for a variety of purposes, not least in ameliorating human suffering.

5

The human genome and theological issues

Peter Manley Scott

> Miranda: How came we ashore?
> Prospero: By providence divine.
>
> *The Tempest,* I.2

Introduction

In Chapter 1, we learned a little about the human genome and genetic science, and were introduced to some of the key themes that run throughout this chapter and the whole book. In Chapter 2 we explored some of the issues raised by the mapping of the human genome through a consideration of five case studies. In the previous chapter we considered the 'secular' discussion on ethical matters concerned with the human genome. For Christians, such 'secular' exploration is important. So in this chapter we begin with a brief theological engagement with this secular discussion before moving into a constructive theological discussion. Thereafter we consider issues of naturalness, life, genetic reductionism, and social justice, before concluding with a presentation of a theological vision of the human for an age of genetic science.

Engaging the secular discussion

How should Christian churches respond to the secular discussion carefully presented in Chapter 4? This is not an easy question to answer. Why not? Any response to the secular discussion must grant some *standing* to the secular discussion. But what precisely is this standing?

Two extremes present themselves at this point. At one extreme, it is tempting to claim that the secular discussion proceeds – by common definition – without reference to God. In other words, theology must seek to *displace* this discussion; 'secular' here comes close to meaning 'false'. And we should note immediately that such an approach is often very illuminating and may disclose the ways in which secular discourse has religious undertones and sets itself up as a salvific discourse. At the other extreme, theology acknowledges that *public* discourse is now secular discourse, and so theology must work with the secular. In effect, there is no other game in town, and if theology wishes to be heard 'publicly' then it will need to work with – if not always accept – such secular discourse. And we should note immediately the strength and theological pedigree of this attempt by theology to engage with other meanings and commitments. (We may also note here that the persistent temptation for an *established* Church is to gravitate towards the second of these extremes and thereby chase after a public role.)

This book does not begin from one extreme or the other but, guided by the subject matter of genomic science, draws on both approaches. This is the case not least because it notes the historical contribution of Christianity to the emergence of the secular and that our present secular society still bears traces of its Christian inheritance. Yet, it considers that the present commitment to healing and health is also part of a Christian inheritance and might be reconsidered by fresh reference to that inheritance. Moreover, there are ambiguities and weaknesses in the traditions of theological thinking that invite a caution about claiming too confidently that weaknesses in secular discourses can be directly and easily repaired by Christian thinking. Theology must be both bold and cautious, but not in equal measure.

A glance back at Chapter 4 will enable us to put some flesh on these dry methodological bones. In one way, secular bioethics might be grasped as an opportunity for the Church in that there already exists a significant public discussion. Yet it is unlikely that the Church can leave the matter there. Recall, for example, that the chapter opens with a discussion of commodification and argues that a thing becomes a commodity through exchange, and that markets are not impersonal. At this point, we may think – with some justification – that theology has little to offer because theology has tended not to concern itself with such social issues. Yet recent theological efforts in developing notions of 'structural sin' might helpfully be referred to here. And we might then move to a renewed consideration of the *production* of commodities rather than only their exchange. As such, we might wish to conclude that commodification and the market are less benign than bioethics often maintains. Whether such an analysis that draws on the concept of sin is convincing, and how such discourse might play in the public realm, are of course matters that need attention.

Theology may also wish to *add* considerations to an ethical discussion regarding the use of genetic materials. At this point, the way the debate is set up can easily paint theology into a corner. For example, to use language that sets up the claim that manipulating genes is inherently wrong and that genes should never be manipulated forces theology into an all-or-nothing position. Are you with us or against us? Rather, theology might refuse the polarized way in which the debate is constructed and *add* a view of human flourishing. In other words, it insists that these developments must be measured against a theological vision of the human.

And as for consideration of the extent to which the non-human might be manipulated, theology might propose that there *is* a difference between the changes secured by way of selective breeding on the one hand and genetic manipulation on the other. Rather than accepting that the 'natural order' can be altered, theology might prefer to think in terms of the stability of natural forms conferred in and by time. At its best, therefore, theology does not claim that the natural is fixed but rather enjoys an alterable stability through time. The patience exhibited by selective breeding is, in this perspective, not similar to the impatience for change demonstrated by genetic manipulation. And theology might thereafter propose that such patience makes a contribution to the flourishing of the human and the non-human.

There are no ready-made responses or knock-down arguments in these discussions. All that is being suggested here is that clarity arrived at in a hurry may not be clarity at all. Perhaps at root here are competing conceptions of the human such that ready agreement should not be expected. Nonetheless, the point is not that revelation corrects reason but that there are different ways of posing the ethical issues emerging from the human genome and thereby sometimes a failure to agree on what the ethical issues are. Indeed, on occasion what theology may find troubling is the certainty with which answers are given.

That secular discussion has colonized the public discussion will be of concern to Christian communities. Nonetheless, that there is such a secular discussion at all is to be welcomed by Christian communities not least because this helps to support the durability of ethical exchange. And such durability is not to be taken lightly nor hurriedly cast aside. Not least, Christian communities have a major investment in the quality of moral conversation and to the extent that secular bioethics makes a contribution to that, the Church will welcome it.

Constructive theological engagement

As already noted, for Christians such secular exploration is important. Yet for Christians it is hardly sufficient. Although theological issues were broached in Chapter 1 we need now to explore these theological issues in more depth. Through the next few sections, we shall move from general to specific issues, concluding with a discussion of human beings as being made in the image of God and becoming more fully in the image of God. Of course, in common with many others, Christians hope for – and work for – a good outcome in history. However well informed by other disciplines and perspectives, nonetheless the decisions that Christians come to regarding the human genome will be *theological* decisions. To this theological work we now turn.

The term 'commodification' has already been introduced. Commodification conveys a negative judgement on the mapping of the human genome. Thus any theology of the human genome will need to address the negative issues associated with commodification: the turning of the human genome into a commodity to be commercialized and exploited and a consequent concern that the human is also being commercialized and exploited.

Commodification is at the heart of genetic science. Consider this opening of a newspaper report on the development of a genetic database of microbes: '[T]he project will compile a huge genetic library that will teach scientists how living things are put together and help them to harness novel genes for creating new drugs or pollution-free energy.'[1]

Furthermore, we will need carefully to discuss the issue of medical tests and therapies that may follow as a result of the knowledge derived from the mapping of the human genome. Who will develop these diagnostic tests and therapies, who will have control over their use, and what will be the cost (financial and other) to the user of these diagnostic tests and therapies? Trying to answer these questions will occupy us through this chapter and some of the other chapters.

However, our approach will not only be negative. That is, we shall not only be attentive to how processes of commodification thwart the purposes of God and restrict the freedom of God to be God in the technological ways of the world. Put differently, the Christian Churches are strongly invested in overcoming physical suffering. The Churches have taken a cue from the reports in the Gospels of Jesus' healing miracles. 'Jesus Christ Himself spent a remarkable fraction of his brief time on earth healing the sick.'[2] And the history of the Churches' role in establishing hospitals is an honourable one.[3] Thus we must also explore the possibility that there is a positive case to be made here. How shall we understand the goodness of God in this context, and how is this goodness distributed through our technology? What is a righteous and justice-making response to the mapping of the human genome, and how might this response be understood as conforming to God's presence and work with us?

The mapping, commodification and commercialization of the human genome raise general and specific issues for theology. Let's start with some general issues.

Getting oriented

First, technology requires us to think about change. Of course, we must think about change at the level of technology: will the information gathered by the mapping of the human genome permit technological advances? Will new techniques be developed, and will older medical techniques be made more precise and effective? However, we need also to consider change at a social level. Above all, we need to consider what sort of change we want – of what sort of change do we approve? (And who are the 'we' here?) In turn, the issue of the society and change invokes a *vision of the human*. Against what vision of the human do we wish to measure and judge change?

A vision of the human sounds a little grand. However, we can concretize this by asking the question: what vision of the human are we being offered today? One image that may be a useful caricature here is that of the lycra-clad athlete. Think of the professional cyclist clad to head to foot in a wind-reducing, skin-tight outfit, designed to maximize speed and reduce resistance. On this analogy, technology here functions as a second skin that insulates us from our context and that permits us to speed through our circumstance: onward, always onward! Here technology improves our ability to insulate ourselves from life, to enable us to reshape our bodies into efficient, sleek human-machines travelling with least impediment across environments.

Of course, whether such a vision of the human is theologically acceptable requires further discussion; we'll return to the issue of a theological vision of the human at the end of this chapter. For the moment, let us note technology functioning as a sort of second skin insulating us from our environment – is that the way we wish to think of the purpose of new developments in medical technologies? How much hope should we invest in medicine, and what should our attitude to medical treatments be? According to US theologian Gerald P. McKenny, questions such as these were raised in classical times by the philosopher Plato: 'What limits should we observe in our efforts to improve our bodily performance and remove causes of suffering?'[4] Yet this question is not much attended to now. Given this sort of vision of the human, we can readily appreciate why moral theologian Robert Song argues that the mapping of the human genome functions as a sort of soteriological project by promising 'the elimination of suffering and the maximisation of individual choice'.[5] And an irony persists here: failure to respond to McKenny's and Song's reservations ensures that our dependence on these medical developments goes uncriticized: technologies may promise to set us free but they may also enslave us to unsupportable and harmful visions of the human.

Second, what should a Christian's attitude to genetic technology be? This question is important because information derived from the human genome informs new medical tests, putative therapies and genetics/population studies. In other words, new medical tools or technologies are in prospect. Some theologians argue that the Church tends to offer two responses to technology: technology as benign, or technology as apocalyptic.

Neither of these responses is satisfactory. The first insulates technology from human sinning and thereby deems technological development as somehow exceptional in its ability to escape from human wickedness. (The Human Genome Project offered a version of this: distinguishing mapping procedures from ethical, legal and social issues.) The second considers technology to be only of the devil and part of a culture that is entering a crisis and will shortly be closing down. As this is a misunderstanding of Christian apocalyptic – such apocalyptic features a God who closes in, not a god who closes down – such an approach lacks credibility. We shall therefore need a more considered response to technological developments and technological change than these two options.

Finally, the phrase 'playing God' is much bandied about in this context. According to Ted Peters, the phrase has three meanings, only one of which concerns us here: 'the use of science to *alter life and influence human evolution*'.[6] In other words, human beings through genetic research and genetics-based medicine are altering human nature. Such alteration is God's prerogative, and so human beings are thereby understood to be 'playing God'. Obviously the phrase cannot mean putting ourselves in the place of God, as if we could somehow understand ourselves as ungenerate creativity! Instead, some implicit notion of limit is being invoked here: that as human creatures we are bounded, and our DNA somehow gives our boundedness.

To mess with these limits is therefore to misuse our knowledge and claim a moral wisdom that we do not have. One way of putting this is to say that our DNA is sacred.

Although Christians as well as others have deployed this phrase, 'playing God', it is theologically unconvincing. How so? First, it requires us to affirm the givenness of the present order in an unhelpful way. Not least, the relationship proposed between God and human nature could require us to make no changes whatsoever: that which is given by God should not be altered. In the face of medical suffering, this seems a rather odd option. Would it not be immoral to accept all givenness, especially that of physical suffering? As Scottish theologian Ruth Page puts the matter: '[I]f the wisdom and knowledge of God in ordering creation is the decisive matter on the Christian side, these have not prevented such anomalies as Siamese twins, or people born with the gene for Huntington's chorea.'[7]

Second, to invoke human DNA as sacred cuts against a theological affirmation of the difference between creator and creation, and the desacralization that this difference requires. In other words, deep in Christian tradition is the claim that creature and creator are *different*. In light of this claim, we should be suspicious of efforts to breach this difference and associate the creaturely with the sacred.

If we refuse the connection between genes and sacredness, are we then without any guidance in this matter? A better guide here might be the sacraments. For water, bread and wine to function as sacraments – as material intensifications of God's blessing towards creatures – requires the theological view that all creation participates in God and is resourced by God's blessing. It is not necessary to invoke the language of 'the sacred' to make this point.

The phrase 'playing God' is therefore unconvincing. However, it must be emphasized that *nothing follows from this*. In other words, although we are not playing God, this does not mean that we have permission to manipulate our DNA. Different, and better, theological arguments must be found to help us explore the lack of wisdom in the manipulation of human DNA.

From this discussion, we learn that to develop a theology for the human genome we shall refuse summary phrases such as 'playing God' and we should not confuse a theological response to technology with the refusal of all technology. Moreover, to develop a positive assessment of the human genome we shall be guided by a theological vision of the human and its flourishing. In short, we shall require an ecclesial and social vision of the human.

Naturalness

We come to our first specific theological issue: naturalness. We can best approach this issue of naturalness if we note the importance for theology of *order*.[8] Whether we refer to God's creating, liberating or redeeming, always presupposed is an order.

> In creating, God gives life;
> in liberating, God saves people in specific situations;
> in redeeming, God transforms, that is, changes already established forms.

Through all of God's action, something is given; there are definite creaturely shapes, however far these shapes are from the *telos* in the kingdom. In that there are two possible attitudes here the next step is crucial. Should we say that the God-given order should not be altered and that any such actions are unnatural and immoral? Or should we take a more activist line and argue that actions that redesign creation towards the amelioration of suffering should be encouraged?[9] In that the human is both subject and object – we regard our bodies as objects as well as subjects – it seems very difficult to maintain the first option.

Especially if taking the first option, it is tempting at this point to associate this givenness with naturalness. In other words, to claim that wherever we are in providence that it is always possible faintly to discern the outlines of a God-given order. This givenness is then cast in a theological idiom and renamed creatureliness. As an example, I have in front of me an issue of *The Watchtower* that stresses the different yet complementary roles of a man and woman in marriage. One caption reads, with italics added: 'Man and woman are *designed* to occupy dignified roles in God's *arrangement*.'[10]

We might call this approach 'romantic': a standard of naturalness 'beyond' culture is asserted against which technological innovation must be tested. And this naturalness is then understood as God-given. Such an approach might argue that the human genome is natural or given and therefore should not be improved in any way. Part of the stability of the world, so this argument runs, is given to us through the genetic basis of our bodies, and that stability should not be messed with. Naturalness is here granted moral authority. And naturalness is sourced to the creatureliness that is in turn given by God.

Of course this is not the only way in which naturalness can be deployed. Indeed, this 'romantic' option is the minority report. In this minority report, nature functions as the criticism of technological culture.

A more common route is in contrast to understand culture as the critic of nature. So let's consider this second option. Of course, naturalness still functions as sort of given but such givenness is taken up into culture and can be changed through cultural practices. Christian communities are not obliged to accept such naturalness. Theological justification for genetic manipulation can be found here. Whereas in the first option naturalness is associated with creation, in this option culture is associated with redemption.[11]

Another theological position – a third option – may be possible, and it is the stance taken throughout this book. Both of the two options set out above rely on the inertness of nature. That is, naturalness is either deployed in criticism of culture or naturalness is deemed to be that which is to be corrected and improved. As regards the theological standing of nature, both options are theologically anaemic. Putting a little iron into these theological positions means freeing ourselves from the view that nature – including human bodies – is inert. Theologically, there is little reason to hold to the view that nature is inert. In creation, God creates the human *with* non-human nature; in salvation, God frees us for an *embodied* life; and in redemption, God seeks the fulfilment of the human *with* nature. Christianity is not Gnostic.

Given this theological orientation, the human is not opposed to nature and nor does the human seek to correspond more fully to a given nature. Creatureliness, both human and natural, is interactive and dynamic. We shall return to this more dynamic account in the final section as we seek to sketch a theology of the human genome. Not least, such a ferrous theology of the human genome will criticize the commercialization and iniquitous exploitation of genomic science.

Life as non-exploitable and non-patentable?

Making a distinction between that which is living and that which is not living is useful in refusing the commodification of the human genome. How does the distinction operate in this context?

That what is not living can be commercialized and exploited seems unremarkable. The history of patenting is a good example of a tradition of securing some legal control over new materials, techniques or knowledge. Patenting tries to draw the distinction between the natural and the artificial. In effect, a Lockean account of property is operative here: once that which is natural has had human labour mixed with it, it is now understood to be artificial, a work of human hands, and thereby in principle open for commodification and – also perhaps, given specific conditions – patentable.

The problem here is that the human genome is living: it resources and shapes living bodies. Its commodification, and thereafter its patenting, are therefore problematic in that life is qualitatively different from non-life. The God of life is the source of the human and the natural and the source of life in both. That which is living can therefore never be regarded as only artificial and so cannot be treated as patentable.

The theological position articulated in *God, ethics and the human genome* presents a prior distinction: that between God and God's creatures. God bestows life and therefore creaturely life has a special status: it has an intrinsic relationship to God. God's life *pro nobis* is most fully present in the liveliest life of this world. As such, life is not patentable.

Genetic reductionism

If we accept that that which is living is not patentable, and therefore that the human genome is not patentable, we must now explore two further problems. In the next section we shall explore the relationship between medical therapies and justice. In this section, we shall explore the matter of 'genetic reductionism'.

The reduction of specific human actions to their genetic basis has been much discussed in the media. Is there a 'gay gene', for instance, or is there a gene whose trait bestows a propensity to violence? If the answer to both these questions is yes, what would be the point of some Christian efforts to 'cure' gay people of their homosexuality and could a gene-based tendency towards violence be offered as a mitigating circumstance in a court of law? Genetic scientists are of course sceptical about such popularizations of their work. Yet reducing human action to its genetic basis has attracted enough attention for it to be discussed here.

Let's begin by noting that genetic science is based in the current pre-eminence of molecular biology. In itself this state of affairs is unproblematic. This state of affairs only becomes problematic if the level of the molecular is taken as the primary explanatory level. As social theorist Bronislaw Szerszynski puts this matter: 'The dominance of molecular biology, with its strongly reductionistic aspirations, threatens a reordering of the sciences, as human behaviour is seen as reducible to biology, and biology to physics and chemistry.'[12] If such reordering were to be widely accepted then primacy would be given to mathematical computation in interpreting the human (that's you and me!).

What is theologically troubling about this? Following this logic, we could argue, with theologian Maureen Junker-Kenny, that 'the HGP implicitly . . . tends to reduce the human person to the sum of her genes'.[13] Once more, we see that the logic of this version of genetic science is reductionist: it seeks to explore the complex by reference to the simple – indeed, to that which is deemed to be a sort of monocausal action: the gene.

Moreover, following Junker-Kenny, it is vital to grasp that we are being offered a geneticized vision of the human that stresses, among other things, objectification, predetermination, autonomy as choosing, progress, control and perfectibility, and the elimination of suffering. These aspects might be contrasted with more directly theological emphases, correspondingly: self-reflection, freedom, autonomy as self-legislation before the divine, finitude, spontaneity, fallibility and being somewhat accepting of human fragility and suffering.[14]

Given these contrasting accounts of the human, we may now appreciate that an oft-quoted question, 'Is God in our genes?', needs careful thought. What does the question mean? Presumably the question does not mean to imply that God is in the space of our genes. That would be foolishness. Perhaps it might be better to say that what is meant is that God reaches us by way of our genes. What does that mean, however? We have no direct experience of the operations of our genes on us except to the extent that their *effects* may be grasped by our reflective consciousness. And we cannot be sure that we are interpreting these effects correctly.

Of course, we have information from the mapping of the human genome. However, how is that information to be interpreted – should it be interpreted by deploying the same framework that produced that information, or by another framework? In other words, should information that is produced by referring the complex to the simpler be interpreted by reference to the same procedure? For the present, perhaps all that needs to be said is that to the extent that actions of genes contribute to the stability of the world, including the human world, then genes are one of the ways by which God confers God's blessing.

Medical therapies and social/medical justice

The refusal of genetic reductionism raises once more the issue of the level at which the human genome is interpreted. Put differently, we might agree that information gleaned through the mapping of the human genome may be used for medical, therapeutic purposes. However, is this the level or context in which this information is best interpreted? Are we invited also to refer the assumed benefits of medical practices to other sorts of benefit? If we should affirm some genomic solidarity among and between humans, are there also other forms of solidarity – political, social and economic – that should be invoked here? Of immense interest here is the way in which the human genome is invoked as a form of solidarity: the 1997 *Universal Declaration on the Human Genome and Human Rights* considers the human genome as underpinning 'the fundamental unity of all members of the human family' and as such 'the common heritage of the human family'.[15]

What follows from this? We must consider the broader context in which medical therapies emerge and are administered, especially the context of the health of a society. In the ordering of health priorities, what priority is to be given to the information gleaned from the mapping of the human genome, and how does this relate to other priorities?

For example, what about preventing diseases and changing the circumstances that give rise to disease – rather than only curing disease? What priority should be given to such imperatives? As Robert Song puts the matter:

> [C]an money spent on this project finally be justified in a world where many are suffering and dying of diseases or other causes which are already much more treatable? Who is likely to benefit most in the short, medium and long terms – and how should we ensure equitable distribution of the fruits of the research?[16]

And if this view still seems too Eurocentric, consider the following comment by US theologian Lisa Sowle Cahill: 'Right now, clean water, food, basic health care, perinatal care, and the AIDS pandemic are of mightier concern in most cultures than genomics.'[17]

We keep returning to the issue of *how* to interpret genomic information, and whether there should be some moral direction given to the use of such information. Of course, we are encroaching on the extended ethical discussion of these issues in Chapter 4. However, for now, we may insist that the 'fundamentalist' interpretation of science is here ruled out. (And it must be noted that most scientists do not hold such a fundamentalist interpretation.) Such a fundamentalist interpretation argues that science is self-interpreting, along the lines of 'Science says . . .' In contrast, this chapter's discussion recommends that genomic science raises questions on which Christianity will wish to comment, clustered around such issues as the goodness of God, the identity of the human and the idolatry of scientific practice. On this view, science may propose but the Christian will always wish to pose questions regarding the salvation of God, the understanding of the human self and the pretensions of knowledge (including scientific knowledge).

A theological vision of the human: *imago dei* and 'genomic solidarity'

So far we have explored the distinction between life and non-life and the problem of reducing the human to its genetic basis and the moral issue of equity and medical therapies. Is it possible to comprehend these three issues by reference to a single theological reference point? The obvious candidate here is the image of God (*imago dei*). What then might this theological vision of the human look like?

What can the *imago dei* do – what argument may it sustain? It may refer us to some attribute or capacity of humanity – reason, freedom, intelligence, tool making, language, creativity or personality. Or, it may refer us to action and relationship: not 'image of God', but the vocation of *imaging God*.

It can support genomic solidarity by insisting that all humans share in the *imago*. This is welcome in a situation in which a competitive race is being constructed over the quality of genes. So the language of *imago dei* is used here to ensure that no group of humans is excluded. However, being in the image of God is not required to make this case; a version of natural rights would do just as well. We need more here than a procedural point: that all humans are bound together in genomic solidarity on account of an inheritance of imaging God held in common.

There are further problems here with the concept of *imago dei*. This approach tends to stress the difference between the human and the non-human – and yet the findings of the mapping of the human genome recommend the view that 99 per cent of human genes are shared with the higher apes. Moreover, it is not clear how the difference between the human and the other is to be marked. And whatever this difference is, it must somehow be universal and preparatory for Christ – all human beings must participate in it and it must help Christians to identify Jesus as the Messiah. Furthermore, it must not trade upon the inertness of nature. Let's begin with the human before moving on to consider the matter of the Incarnation.

We might attend to overcoming the inertness of nature by stressing that there is a link between the 'mastery' of nature and overcoming the contingency of human bodies. Our desire to render passive the non-human is mimicked in our desire to pacify the suffering of our bodies. We are agents; the non-human, and our objectified bodies, are not.

We do not have to view the matter this way. Indeed, we can enjoy a different picture if we affirm that God reaches us by way of non-human and human bodies. Of course, it is not true that God is *in* our genes anymore than it is sensible to say that God is *in* the process of evolution. However, it is also true that God works through these secondary causes; God is present to – rather than in – these secondary causes, and it is by way of these processes and causes that God continues to create, liberate and redeem. Our vocation is therefore not to dominate but at least in part to receive the blessings of God as God recruits us by way of bodies, others' and ours.

What is it that links us to other bodies? One way of thinking about this is to maintain that we are in an embodied society with others and with animals. Animals form communities with their own kind. Yet we are joined together – community by community – by social bonds: a commonwealth of sociality. From here it would be a piece of orthodox theo-logic to argue that the triune God is the giver of this sociality – its origin, form and movement. This means that bodies are bound together with a definite shape and yet with a certain direction. Bodies are always bodies through change, and yet through these changes bodies are never independent.

On this schema, the Incarnation of God in the human can be justified if in some ways the human is universal: that is, seen as the summary of all creation. The human capacity to be social must be of a greater intensity than that of other creatures but also quantitatively linked to others. Of course, this intensity has a genetic basis: it is in 'the complexity of their multiple interactions' that genes resource human, social interaction.[18] On this view the *imago dei* is less a state of being – and certainly not a genetically determined state of being – but more of a vocation: a sort of pedagogy. Imaging God directs us to the horizon of the creative action of God thereby referring us beyond ourselves. We are social beings, turned outwards. This turning outward in social freedom is resourced by the action of God and is the way in which God encounters us.

On this view, the struggle for health is a kind of vocation: health is a kind of calling, through which God reaches us as creatures through our freedom.[19] Yet such a calling occurs only in a specific social context. Christian communities will therefore be attentive to the social contexts in which such a call is received.

Genetic information must therefore be referred to its wider social context of production. Transcendence means that we should struggle against illness, but we require political and social conditions that support that struggle. If it is by way of social embodiment that the call for health reaches us, that call will be restricted through the unfreedom of any situation. Moreover, the work for good health will be a sort of social *struggle* through the social distortions of any situation. As such, human genes are only human genes in sociality. The interpretation of genes will therefore be affected by distortions in that context, including tendencies towards commodification. And if sociality identifies us as creatures, ill health is also part of our creaturely condition and orientation towards death, and so cannot finally be defeated. In turn, we should be suspicious of any who promise us such a defeat. Only *creaturely* struggle is recommended.

Given this theological vision of the human, how are social and legal issues to be assessed? And what is the work of the Church? The next two chapters explore answers to these questions. However, there is no doubting the difficulty in coming to wise moral judgements in this area. Nor is there any doubting the obligation laid on the Church to be a witness to that resourcing by the freedom of God, and an opponent of its distortions; to be a champion of creation's goodness, and an opponent of its distortions.

6

A brief legal interlude: intellectual property and patent protection

John Overton

What is a patent?

The purpose of this section is to bring the reader, whose understanding of what a patent is may be not much more than that of someone who has seen 'Patent No. X,XXX,XXX' on a warm-air hand drier in a public convenience, to an informed position of knowing (1) what a patent is (and, very importantly, what it is *not*), (2) how we have got to the kind of patent system that we have at present, (3) how to read a patent specification, and (4) how to determine in a debate whether patents are *the* issue, a major issue, are peripheral to some more important issue or are irrelevant because the speaker or writer appears to be misinformed.

1. Intellectual property – patents

Patents are a subset of what nowadays is usually referred to as 'intellectual property'. Intellectual property is an umbrella term which includes patents, utility models, plant variety protection, supplementary protection certificates (for medicinal products and plant protection products), registered designs, copyright, trademarks (registered and unregistered), know-how and trade secrets (this is not an exhaustive list).

As a form of property, a patent can be assigned, sold, mortgaged, licensed, given away, or allowed to lapse.

A patent is a form of monopoly, granted for a limited period of time (a typical maximum term is 20 years) for a defined area of technology. **It is an *exclusive* right, i.e. a right to exclude others from doing what is covered by the patent, and *not* a positive right to do what is covered by the patent.** This is a most important fact to keep in mind, and one to which we shall return.

Patents differ from copyright in that they are infringed by anything falling within their scope, whereas a person's copyright is infringed only if actual copying has occurred. Where something has been completely independently devised, there can be no infringement of copyright.

There is no direct basis in the Bible for patents, but once we admit that 'any thing that is thy neighbour's' in the prohibition against coveting in the Tenth Commandment (Exodus 20.17 (RV)) includes the products of one's neighbour's ingenuity, laws such as patent laws can be seen to be consistent with biblical principles.

2. How have we reached today's patent system?

British patent law was, until the Patents Act 1977, based on Section 6 of the Statute of Monopolies 1623, and it is worth reproducing the text of that section here.

> 6. Provided also, that any declaration before mentioned shall not extend to any letters patents and grants of privilege for the term of fourteen years or under, hereafter to be made, of the sole working or making of any manner of new manufactures within this realm to the true and first inventor and inventors of such manufactures, which others at the time of making such letters patents and grants shall not use, so as also they be not contrary to the law nor mischievous to the state by raising prices of commodities at home, or hurt of trade, or generally inconvenient:
>
> the same fourteen years to be accounted from the date of the first letters patents or grant of such privilege hereafter to be made, but that the same shall be of such force as they should be if this act had never been made, and of none other.

The Statute of Monopolies 1623 was directed to curbing the power of King James I to grant monopolies, but it was seen as beneficial to make exception in relation to 'new manufactures'. These translate into the basic criteria for patentability today, that in order to be patentable an invention has to be (a) novel (new, in relation to what is known to be public by virtue of earlier publication or use giving knowledge to the public), (b) inventive (non-obvious, in relation to what is known to be public by virtue of earlier publication or use giving knowledge to the public) and (c) applicable in industry.

The essential bargain between the state and the patentee is that the patentee gets a defined exclusive right in return for a disclosure of the novel and inventive technology, which will enable the public to build on that disclosure (in developing further improved technology) and be able to put the technology into practice generally, once the patent has lapsed or expired.

Patent laws have evolved over time, as technologies and communications have advanced, and as industries moved from a purely national focus to an international focus, and there are still differences between countries' laws.

Novelty and non-obviousness are defined as at the date of filing of a patent application (i.e. what is made known to the public after that date has no effect against the validity of a patent).

The first major international treaty in relation to patents was the Paris Convention of 1883, which provides for the filing date of a patent application made in one Convention country (priority date) to be treated as the effective filing date in another Convention country, provided that any filing in another Convention country is made within a year of the priority date.

Two other major treaties having direct effect on UK patent law are the Patent Cooperation Treaty (PCT) and the European Patent Convention (EPC), both of which came into effect in June 1978.

The PCT allows for filing of a single patent application, designating one or more PCT contracting states. The application becomes published 18 months after its priority date (or filing date, if no priority date is claimed), and passes into the national/regional phase, typically at 30 months from priority date, whereupon it becomes a bundle of national patent applications, which have to be pursued through individual patent offices.

Under the EPC, a single patent application designating one or more EPC states (also published 18 months after its priority date, or filing date, if no priority date is claimed) undergoes search and examination by the European Patent Office (EPO), and upon grant becomes a bundle of national patents, which then have to be enforced in each individual country. For nine months after grant, however, the patent is open to a unitary opposition procedure, whereby interested third parties can seek revocation of the patent on certain specified grounds, which include lack of novelty, lack of inventive step and failure to provide a sufficient disclosure of the invention to enable it to be performed by a skilled reader.

UK patent law is now effectively dominated by the EPC, so that it is no longer possible for the UK to follow an independent line. Similarly, UK law more generally is subject to European Union (EU) Directives.

As indicated above, patent laws have evolved as technologies have developed, and as patent offices and courts have had to apply laws to developments which were not in the mind of legislators when the laws were made. Patent laws usually have a clause prohibiting the patenting of inventions whose exploitation would be contrary to morality. However, what is regarded as contrary to morality in one era (e.g. contraceptives in the UK 50 years ago) may not be considered so at a later time.

Concern about patentability of technology in microbiological and biological developments led to Directive 98/44/EC of the European Parliament and of the Council of 6 July 1998 on the legal protection of biotechnological inventions (http://eur-lex.europa.eu/LexUriServ/LexUriServ.do?uri= CELEX:31998L0044:EN:HTML).

Articles 5 and 6 of this Directive are very pertinent to consideration of the human genome, and read as follows:

Article 5

1. The human body, at the various stages of its formation and development, and the simple discovery of one of its elements, including the sequence or partial sequence of a gene, cannot constitute patentable inventions.

2. An element isolated from the human body or otherwise produced by means of a technical process, including the sequence or partial sequence of a gene, may constitute a patentable invention, even if the structure of that element is identical to that of a natural element.

3. The industrial application of a sequence or a partial sequence of a gene must be disclosed in the patent application.

Article 6

1. Inventions shall be considered unpatentable where their commercial exploitation would be contrary to ordre public or morality; however, exploitation shall not be deemed to be so contrary merely because it is prohibited by law or regulation.

2. On the basis of paragraph 1, the following, in particular, shall be considered unpatentable:

(a)   processes for cloning human beings;

(b)   processes for modifying the germ line genetic identity of human beings;

(c)   uses of human embryos for industrial or commercial purposes;

(d)   processes for modifying the genetic identity of animals which are likely to cause them suffering without any substantial medical benefit to man or animal, and also animals resulting from such processes.

3. How to read a patent specification

A patent specification is both a legal and a technical document, and has to fulfil the essential bargain between the state and the patentee referred to above, in which the patentee gets a defined exclusive right in return for a disclosure of the novel and inventive technology.

Thus a patent specification falls into two essential sections, viz. (i) a description and (ii) claims.

There may be one or more 'claims', which define the technical scope of the monopoly sought (in a patent application) or granted (in a patent). In form, a claim is a continuous statement, ending with a full stop. Historically, it was the object of a sentence beginning 'We claim' or 'What we claim is'. Claims may be independent, or may be dependent upon one or more earlier claims. The function of a dependent claim is to provide 'fall-back' positions in case one or more claims referred to in the dependent claim is invalid.

The description usually begins with a sentence indicating the technical field to which the invention relates. This may be followed by one or more paragraphs referring to prior art disclosures relevant to the background to the invention, and then one or more statements of invention (typically beginning 'According to the invention there is provided . . .' or 'The present invention provides . . .'), which generally mirror the language of the claims. The general description containing the statements of invention is then usually followed by a specific description of one or more embodiments of the invention (which may be headed 'Examples').

When reading a patent specification, it is important to distinguish whether the document is a published patent *application* or a granted patent. The terminology on the front page of the document will usually make this clear, but nowadays a capital 'A' associated with the publication number usually denotes a published application, and a capital 'B' usually denotes a granted patent. Since a patent application will become published provided it meets certain formal requirements and the requisite fees have been paid, its contents may or may not be sound. Publication of a patent application is certainly no guarantee that a patent will eventually be granted.

4. How to determine in a debate whether patents are *the* issue, a major issue, are peripheral to some more important issue or are irrelevant because the speaker or writer appears to be misinformed

As mentioned in Section 1 above, a patent is an *exclusive* right, i.e. a right to exclude others from doing what is covered by the patent, and *not* a positive right to do what is covered by the patent.

What is described in a patent specification can only be commercialized if it is not dominated by one or more earlier patents of third parties, unless a licence is obtained in relation to such earlier rights (e.g. if my patented invention is a hydrogen-filled balloon, and you have an earlier patent covering lighter-than-air balloons, I can only make and sell hydrogen-filled balloons if you license me under your patent).

In fields such as pharmaceuticals, a product can only be put on the market if it has satisfied stringent product registration requirements. Patents are *critically important*, because it only makes economic sense to invest in the basic research and in development and clinical trials if there is exclusivity for long enough to make profits large enough to justify that investment. In such cases, if patents are unavailable, the research and development will not take place.

It can be argued that if something is considered to be an undesirable commercial practice, it does not matter if someone has a patent covering it, because the only legal right conferred by the patent is the right to stop people doing that practice. The most appropriate protest is to lobby to make the practice itself illegal.

In the case of research institutions which are not commercially funded, but which might be likely to indulge in research practices of an undesirable nature, patent laws are likely to be irrelevant to them, and the most appropriate protest is to lobby to make the research practice itself illegal.

The above is intended to serve as a basic introduction to patent issues. Those wanting a more in-depth discussion are recommended to read *The Ethics of Patenting DNA: A Discussion Paper*, Nuffield Council on Bioethics, July 2002. Also at http://www.nuffieldbioethics.org/go/browseablepublications/geneticsandhb/report_354.html.

7

Biotechnology patenting, ethics and theology

Donald Bruce

'Where were you, when I laid the foundations of the earth?'

Job 38.4

Introduction

The publishing of the first map of the human genome was heralded as a triumph of scientists working across the globe to unravel our genetic code. The knowledge would now bring widespread benefits to humankind. But when it comes to its lucrative commercial potential, it has often resembled a Wild West gold rush more than twenty-first-century science. Companies, universities and governments have fought, sometimes ruthlessly, to be the first to stake out their gene claims. At the heart of this lies a long-running ethical and political conflict over genetic patents. Should we allow patents on these genes we have identified, or their many applications in medicine, modified organisms, agricultural improvements and so on? Few issues raised by genetics and biotechnology have proved as enduringly controversial.

Patenting is an ethical contract between inventor and society. Society grants the inventor protection for a limited period from anyone else marketing the invention under their own name, in exchange for publishing the full details of the invention. As long as it dealt with ingenious mechanical devices or engineered chemical processes, this was relatively straightforward. The trouble began in the 1980s when patenting began to embrace products of modern biotechnology, such as genes, and modified microorganisms, plants or animals. The assumption was that biological interventions should be subject to the same rules of intellectual property that have long applied to human-made inanimate objects, as products of industry rather than of nature. Landmark decisions of the US Supreme Court in 1980 and the US Patent and Trademark

Office in 1987 allowed the patenting of modified living organisms, and in 1991 the National Institutes of Health filed its first patents on sequences of the human genome.[1] Patent lawyer Stephen Crespi expressed the change as follows:

> Historically, the patent system came to birth to meet industrial needs. Industry was perceived as activities carried on inside factories . . . Manufacture was the key word. Agriculture was felt to be outside the realm of patent law. Living things were also assumed to be excluded as being products of nature rather than products of manufacture . . . This restricted view no longer persists in most industrialised countries. Thus the European Patent Convention of 1973 declares agriculture to be a kind of industry. Nevertheless vestiges of the old idea can still be found . . . From the point of view of industrial and social policy, the application of technology to living organisms as industrial tools or products should raise no objection in principle.[2]

This quotation is important in highlighting unspoken value assumptions often made by the patenting profession and the scientific and policy communities. Modernity takes for granted that industrial use must supersede earlier and wider understandings of living things. Objections to patenting genes and living organisms are seen paternalistically as valid 'vestiges of old ideas', failing to recognize the depth of ethical concern, which set the stage for a profound and far-reaching conflict. This came to a head in the protracted negotiations leading to the European Union's 1998 Directive on biotechnology patenting.[3]

The Directive was intended to harmonize European patent legislation, obliging all member states to allow gene patenting. However, it embodied a technical and reductionist logic which was strongly opposed by many in a dispute prefiguring later debates over genetically modified foods. Put simply, when it comes to patenting, there is no essential difference between a mouse trap and a genetically modified mouse, according to the criteria used by industry and commerce. But the European Churches and many civil society groups maintained that there are important moral distinctions which are denied if only narrow legal and scientific criteria are taken into account. The conflict is well illustrated by a response of the European Commission's research directorate to the Churches' concerns. It stated that 'the ethical perspective must not *a priori* interfere with the objective approach of patent law by introducing elements which are alien to it'. Yet only a month before, the European Commission's own ethical advisory group argued that when biological material was involved, the ethical dimension became a central factor.[4]

Genetic patenting and the Churches

A number of churches have actively addressed biotechnology patenting. The most significant role was by the bioethics working group of the European Ecumenical Commission for Church and Society (EECCS)[5] (now united with the Conference of European Churches, CEC), which made a series of submissions to the European Commission and the European Parliament,[6] by the Church of Scotland Society, Religion and Technology Project, the Society of Friends (Quakers), the German Protestant Church (EKD) and the US United Methodist Church. There have also been significant initiatives by the UK Methodist Church and by the Canadian Council of Churches.

From 1991 to 1995 the UK Methodist Church ran a series of annual conferences on genetics at Luton Industrial College, which included well-informed discussions on patenting. This was followed by a booklet on genetics,[7] and a discussion pack for churches.[8] The most in-depth study of the field has been by the Society, Religion and Technology Project (SRT) of the Church of Scotland. An expert working group with several leading geneticists examined genetic modification in non-human life forms between 1993 and 1998, published as the influential book *Engineering Genesis*, with a detailed chapter on patenting issues,[9] and a series of reports to the General Assembly.[10] The SRT Project has also contributed to international discussions on patenting with bodies such as UNESCO, the International Association for the Protection of Intellectual Property (AIPPI) and the UK Chartered Institute of Patent Agents. The respective theological pros and cons of gene patenting were also addressed by Reiss and Bruce.[11] The German EKD churches also have a long history of engagement on patenting issues. The Church of England Board of Social Responsibility has addressed human and non-human genetic issues many times, but the Church has not published more specifically on patenting until this present initiative.

An important question is *how* the Churches should engage on such a complex technical issue. In her study on religious engagement in genetics,[12] Audrey Chapman contrasted a well-publicized statement against biotechnology patents by US religious leaders in 1995, and the EECCS European Churches' engagement with the EC Directive. She criticized the US statement because it did not build on existing and consistent concerns within the issues in the Churches, was long after the key events, and represented too uncritical an endorsement of the views of a secular environmental campaigner. In contrast, EECCS drew on existing expertise and reflection within the Churches, and engaged in timely fashion with the key European legislation, making concrete recommendations.

The Society of Friends is active on the impact on developing countries of patenting aspects of World Trade Organization (WTO) agreements. Geoff Tansey has worked extensively on the subject for the Quaker United Nations Office in Geneva, which has produced authoritative publications.[13] They and the SRT Project helped the Catholic International Cooperation for Development and Solidarity (CIDSE) to produce a report on patenting in relation to food security.[14] To discuss the complex ethical concerns of gene patenting for developing countries would take a chapter on its own. Suffice to say that the Trade-Related Aspects of Intellectual Property Rights Agreement (TRIPS) requires that all inventions be patentable, including those that are based on the exploitation of biological resources. Article 27.3(b) exempts plant and animals (but not microorganisms) but still requires some form of intellectual property protection for new plant varieties. Although countries are free to determine their own systems, negotiations are highly unequal. Tansey likens it to Manchester United playing downhill, against a team only some of whom are professionals, and some of whom have never played soccer before. For example, it is hard to treat issues such as medicines or genetic resources on their merits. They may be compromised in trade-offs over other aspects of WTO negotiations, or overriden by bilateral agreements, in which an industrial country may impose on the poorer country more stringent conditions about intellectual property or the use of materials than are required in the TRIPS agreement. A widespread concern is that many such agreements represent for the poor country an unwelcome imposition of industrialized agriculture, the power of foreign multinational companies, and the privatization of knowledge, at the expense of traditional systems and indigenous concepts of communal property.

Ethical and theological issues of biotechnology patenting

Biotechnology patenting raises a complex array of questions. Firstly there is an important general question about the place of ethics in patenting itself. This leads secondly to the major theological issues. Should living organisms and certain types of biological material such as genes be regarded as patentable or do they represent a different category from inanimate matter? An important question is *what* has truly been invented, as opposed to simply discovered, or is part of a much larger system? If we exempt from patenting human genes or modified living organisms *in themselves*, may we still patent applications which make *use of* them? Then there are a range of ethical problems about how biotechnology patenting operates in practice, which includes whether it is good or bad for society to grant monopoly rights for certain basic sorts of invention. Finally there are concerns about how patenting applies in poor and developing countries.

1. What have ethical issues got to do with patenting?

The essentials of patenting are described more fully in Chapter 6. Within the scientific and patent law communities, patenting is generally seen as a purely legal process. It is assessed by experienced examiners, according to rules laid down in the relevant patent law, such as the EU Directive and the European Patent Convention, following procedures of assessment built up over centuries. Patent lawyers frequently assert that the ethical implications of a patent are not their business, because whether something can be patented is a technical procedure within law, and not a matter of ethics. If there are ethical issues to do with the invention itself, these are properly dealt with by the relevant national regulatory authorities not the patent offices. Here lies the first of many clashes of viewpoint.

This view of the intellectual property process denies the obvious. All human activities have an ethical dimension, including patenting. The very concept of a patent embodies a balance between two competing ethical 'goods'. One is open access to information for the widest benefit of society. The second is the right of any individual or group in society to benefit financially from their inventiveness. More specifically, the ethical dimension is expressly recognized in the EU Directive and the European Patent Convention, in that under some circumstances a patent may be refused if its publication or the use of the invention were seen to be 'contrary to ordre public or morality'.[15] Finally, as observed above, the EC's own ethical advisors saw that the ethical dimension is a central issue in biotechnology patenting.

The EC ethical advisory group also noted, however, that the patent process is not the best place to examine such ethical issues. Patent agents are under a professional obligation to patent unless there is a technical reason not to do so. Patent examiners are not trained in ethics nor would their closed deliberations easily be held accountable to civil society on whose behalf they were making judgements. These are fair points. Moreover, it may create an ironic situation. A rare example of the refusal of a patent clause on ethical grounds was the claim for the use of a hairless mouse for research into the treatment of baldness. This was rejected as too trivial a use of an animal. To deny the patent did not mean that the applicants were forbidden to use the mouse for this purpose, but only that they could not prevent anyone else from doing it.

But the reality is that until the patent has been filed, the very rules of patenting forbid any kind of disclosure, and thus any external ethical analysis or public discussion. It is usually only once the patent is filed that the public or ethical experts become aware of the invention. It seems rather late to wait this long to assess the ethics of the invention itself. The problem is that there is generally no parallel system for the ethical assessment of an invention itself which would make it illegal to make an unethical invention, and would also automatically forbid a patent on it. The European Churches proposed that an independent ethical body was needed to assess the ethics of particularly sensitive inventions for which a patent application had been filed. An amendment was proposed by a member of the European Parliament but the EC claimed that the existence of its ethical advisory group satisfied this. This was very misleading, because the terms of reference and resourcing of this group preclude addressing more than broad policy areas. It could never consider individual patent claims. Thus the matter remains unresolved, and some patents continue to attract ethical debate that would be better handled elsewhere.

2. Should we patent living organisms?

The claim that ethics has nothing to do with patenting is further denied by the fact that highly contested fundamental ethical assumptions were built in to the EU directive, namely that living organisms, human genes and biological matter in general should be regarded as patentable.[16] It was taken for granted that if human inventiveness had been applied to them, they were now patentable products of human industry and any previous notion of being products of nature was overriden. This view was not subject to wider public scrutiny or discussion, and was in effect a dogma.

It would be more correct to say that these inventions are products of *both* nature and industry. The values and criteria of both domains should therefore be considered together. The question is then how to handle this hybrid status, and to decide which criteria are the most important.

On the one hand, are biotechnological inventions primarily *industrial* products and processes for which patents generally can be applied for, with a few named exceptions which violate especially important values, such as human cloning? This is the situation in the current EC biotechnology patenting directive. Alternatively, should we regard these primarily as products of *nature*, for which humans may only claim patent protection for specific, novel adaptations? The EECCS submissions and the Church of Scotland argued the latter, on the basis that no one can claim to have invented something that is alive.

People ascribe important values to life forms and aspects of the biosphere. These have to be taken into account, along with the human ingenuity which has modified them. In a Christian understanding, living organisms are God's creations. They and all creation ultimately belong to God, not us. Humans can claim no intellectual property rights over what is merely natural. God has given human beings the dual responsibility to take care of and to develop what God has created, but we are stewards and companions to the creation, not its owners. A special respect is due to any living creature, including humans, because each is ultimately a creation of God. It is a creature in its own right and not something of human invention. Being God's creations, all living organisms have an inherent significance which sets them apart from mere products of human industry.

In Christian ethics, it is argued, the prior ethical criterion is the respect due to living organisms which God has created, which should take precedence over any industrial or other uses to which human beings might think of putting them. It would violate both the respect due to other creatures and the notion of invention if we reckoned that all creatures of a type for which we found a use would be subject to our monopoly, when we did not create these creatures. Because each class of organisms is a creation of God, it is common to all, and its usefulness to humans is common to all. While in human terms I may perhaps 'own' a particular animal, I have no valid claim of monopoly over all other animals of that type.

The Society, Religion and Technology Project's *Engineering Genesis* study expressed the viewpoint that a patent on a living organism might represent an inappropriate commodification:

> The intuition is that this is one further, highly significant step in a process towards regarding living organisms as, in essence, nothing more than biological machines for human utility, with no distinction from inanimate objects . . . Unfortunately, it must also be said that there are enough evidences of misuse of technology, with harm towards both creatures and the environment, to indicate how easy it can be for the product of industry approach, in effect, to take over. There remains an

inherent tension between the two notions, and the opposition to patenting living organisms is to a large degree a response to that tension . . . There need therefore to be reminders in the intellectual property realm, as well as in other areas, that a wholly anthropocentric perspective of utility to humans is insufficient.[17]

3. What has been invented?

A key question is to consider exactly *what* has been invented. In Europe, one cannot patent a mere discovery, which one found in nature or isolated from it. It has to involve an inventive step that was not obvious to anyone else 'skilled in the art'. It also has to have a specified practical or industrial application. If a living creature might be said to have had an inventor, it would presumably be God, or no one. It certainly would not be any particular group of human beings. There is a valid ethical distinction between what is alive and what is not. Something that has a life of its own, like a mouse, cannot be said to be someone's invention, in a way that a mouse trap might be. One may claim a patent on a mouse trap that embodies a novel variation, because the original mouse trap had also been invented. If one modifies a mouse, one cannot claim credit for the pre-existing complexity of a living organism which no one invented.

The European Churches cited the celebrated case of the Harvard oncomouse as an example.[18] This was a type of mouse modified to incorporate a gene of human origin which conferred a susceptibility to a human cancer. The patent claim included not only the novel gene construct but also any mouse containing it. The Churches argued that in no sense did the addition of two or three genes to a mouse justify claiming that the mouse was a human invention. The mouse was a product of nature, a living organism in its own right. The only inventive aspect was the gene construct and its potential uses. From an ethical point of view, it might be acceptable to grant a patent on the novel gene construct to be used in an animal, but not to claim a patent on the transgenic animal itself. This would not violate patent law, would respect wider ethical values about living organisms, and would still grant the inventor practical protection for what they had actually invented.[19]

This prompts the question whether an artificially created organism would be patentable. Using the tools of what has become known as synthetic biology, it might be possible to construct a very simple 'new' organism from constituent sections of DNA. This would presumably be a genuinely human invention, but should a patent be granted to prevent others from making it?

Something with a life of its own is only an invention, however, in so far as the scientist arranged the constituents. Once the concept of the new organism exists, it might be argued that it should not be patentable, because it now has a life in its own right. The process of creating it could be patented but the organism itself should be free of a human monopoly over all other examples of the same type.

4. Should we patent human genes?

The arguments discussed above would suggest that human genes, as naturally occurring in the body, should not be patentable. They are merely discoveries. Although it is now an almost trivial procedure scientifically, it was highly ingenious to identify the first gene sequences. But merely finding out what they are should not entitle the research team to monopoly rights over their use. This is because it is a discovery from nature. Mendeleev could not have claimed a patent on the idea of the then unknown chemical element germanium, whose existence and properties he correctly predicted from his periodic table. The inventiveness would be in a specific use to which the gene was put, not to the gene itself.

At first sight the EC Directive agrees with this:

> Article 5.1. The human body, at the various stages of its formation and development, and the simple discovery of one of its elements, including the sequence or partial sequence of a gene, cannot constitute patentable inventions.

This assertion is, however, largely meaningless because genes within the human body are not used. They are extracted and copied. Thus clause 5.2 asserts that what is involved in patent applications is not the natural genes in the body but so-called 'copy genes', obtained by the technical process of cloning (copying) the original gene millions of times.[20]

> Article 5.2. An element isolated from the human body or otherwise produced by means of a technical process, including the sequence or partial sequence of a gene, may constitute a patentable invention, even if the structure of that element is identical to that of a natural element.

By this clause, the EU hoped to find a way within the European patent system – in which discoveries cannot be patented – to avoid losing out to the US system, in which discoveries like genes *are* patentable. It has been widely criticized as a legal sleight of hand, for several reasons. Firstly, nothing novel or inventive is involved in the process of copying genes. It is a standard biochemical technique. Secondly, the notion of invention is being stretched much too far. The act of using bacteria to make the same combination of atoms that is found in a gene in the human body does not constitute grounds for a commercial monopoly over that human gene sequence. It has the same essential chemical composition as a part of God's creation. Most importantly for the researcher, the human informational content which the gene carries is the same as the original. As the Society, Religion and Technology Project's report observed, 'Many people would regard a copy gene of human origin as remaining "human" because of the way they understand the notion of identity – that it is primarily to do with connections and relationships, not atomised entities.' It is not an invention and should not be patentable.

The Directive in effect also makes an unwarranted distinction between genetic material and other aspects of the human body. In a Christian understanding, human identity is seen as an indissoluble whole, not focused in any one part. There is a fundamental need not to lose sight of the connectedness at the heart of this understanding, in the face of the growing developments in isolating processes of the human body.

It is also argued that it is against a Christian understanding of the nature of the human person, of self-respect and respect for others, that human genetic information should be seen as 'intellectual property'. If the information about a human gene sequence could be said to belong to anyone, it might be the individual concerned, not the geneticist. But it is also shared with other family members, so it is just as much theirs. It is perhaps truer to say that human genes and their informational content are the common property of all humanity, equally. No one is entitled to claim a monopoly over what God has given free to all.

As with living organisms, however, it may be acceptable that inventions involving human genes may be patentable, provided the patent is restricted to a specific use. Thus a testing kit to detect a particular defective genetic sequence might be patentable, but not the gene itself. It is a point of controversy whether the identification of a gene by one person gives them any right to claim prior rights if another inventor should find a use which the discoverer had never thought of. The third clause of Article 5 of the Directive states:

> Article 5.3. The industrial application of a sequence or a partial sequence of a gene must be disclosed in the patent application.

The CEC group asserted that this should be applied rigorously to ensure that no patent on a use of a newly isolated gene sequence prevented any third party from finding another use for it and obtaining their own patent on that use. We have already referred to the unsavoury Gold Rush element of the Human Genome Project. To claim for other uses is tantamount to a claim on the gene itself and would be counterproductive to the aims which the genome project was set up to achieve.

Issues with the practice of patenting

Industry and governments promote patenting as essential to economic growth from science and technology, and a measure of the success of a university, research institute or company. This is based on an ideal of patenting which is, unfortunately, often seriously challenged by the reality of the way it operates in practice. This raises questions of social justice in who wins and loses in the system that has evolved.

A patent application is filed as a series of clauses which describe the invention and express the scope of the protection being sought. A biotechnology invention may be very specific, but it may also seek broad scope of protection. Typically, a patent lawyer will advise the inventor or organization to make claims as wide ranging as possible to maximize benefits. The role of the patent examiner is to check the validity of the claims and to disallow clauses whose scope is unjustified. But an examiner only has a limited time to assess any given claim, under heavy pressure to turn it over very quickly because of the sheer volume of patents. Some outrageous claims of scope have slipped through, such as all forms of modified cotton and Basmati rice. In such cases a third party may have to mount a formal challenge and get the patent re-examined. This can be a lengthy and complex process which only organizations with sufficient resources and expertise are able to do. There seem to be insufficient checks and balances in the patent granting procedures of some jurisdictions, in the face of the inherent tendency for patent lawyers to seek 'as much as they can get away with'.

Nowadays, patenting tends to favour those who are large and powerful. It has moved a long way from its original purpose of protecting individual inventors from unfair commercial use of their ideas. Patenting can work for small organizations, but they also experience disadvantages. The cost of applying for and maintaining a patent annually may be considerable. To present or defend a legal challenge to someone violating one's patent can be prohibitively expensive. Does a small company or institute dare take the risk?

Likewise only the largest civil society organizations have the funds to challenge a patent that they consider to be unethical.

In the world of industrial biotechnology, a company's 'IP' – the patents and other intellectual property rights it holds – is seen as its primary commercial asset, expressing its competitive advantages over its rivals. In the way things have developed, there is a very large amount of time, expense and uncertainty in bringing pharmaceuticals and many other biotechnology products to market, from the initial research discovery. This demands enormous 'up front' investment in research, development and clinical trials, out of which only a very few products will finally reach the market. Most patents on the initial innovation have become de facto insurance to recoup some of this investment, rather than protection for the actual invention, which could still be a decade or more from reaching the market, even if it succeeds. In this sense patents might be said to have lost their purpose somewhat by becoming investment insurance for major companies, which might perhaps be achieved better in other ways.

Patents sometimes hold back beneficial research. A company may hold a broad patent that is designed to keep off their competitors, but unless it maintains its research, the field may wither. There is now much evidence that broad patents on gene sequences or some of the basic techniques involved in genetic modification have held up genetic research and not been a stimulus.[21] Patents are not meant to stop non-profit academic research, but institutions may be less inclined to work in an area where one major player holds key patents. Narrow patents, on the other hand, seem to spawn more research. Complex advances in biotechnology depend on multiple technologies, each governed by different intellectual property. An increasing problem is 'thickets' of several dozen patents, each of which has to have licensing approval from the holder. This has significantly delayed developments of technologies aimed at developing countries' needs. Some companies are belatedly realizing the need to release intellectual property for food and medical needs in developing countries, but the inherent bias in the system remains in protecting the powerful over the poor.

Increasingly, in the complex and lengthy biological processes of discovery, there are grounds to challenge whether it remains fair to reward only the one who happens to be first past the post. The main credit for the intellectual effort, and thus the property which may be claimed from it, may belong to other people and organizations, who nonetheless get no financial reward. Many consider the case of the first breast cancer gene patents to be an abuse of the system. Patenting also has a ratcheting effect. Once one organization raises the stakes on what it is claiming patent protection for, everyone else in the field is under pressure to follow suit or lose competitive advantage.

Even if the conditions of a patent are satisfied, it may not be in society's wider interests to grant monopolies on some inventions. Thus the basic technology of stem cell lines holds great promise in medicine. The CEC bioethics group argued that to grant a monopoly to the first to create such cell lines vests too much power and interest in one organization.[22] Some basic entities like genes and stem cell lines should remain the common property of all rather than the benefit of a few.

Postscript

During the EU Directive discussions, the EECCS group was commended by senior MEPs as a source of balanced and well-informed critique. It had influenced a number of proposed amendments to the Directive. Although most of the amendments fell, under what many observers saw as disturbing circumstances, many of the issues the European Church group raised have become more widely recognized. The notion of patenting genes has been criticized by some senior geneticists, for example Nobel Laureate Sir John Sulston and by the then Director of the Human Genome Institute in Beijing, both of whom were responsible for large parts of the Human Genome Project. Broad patents and rapacious companies have been recognized as hindering research and therapy. The need to keep some things as common has also been realized, and a wider movement for open source publication is having a significant impact.

One of the most significant indicators of change has come from the European Patent Office (EPO). It was the force behind the EU Directive, but began an extensive horizon-scanning exercise in 2006–7 on the technical, economic and social landscape in 2025 and its impact on intellectual property. Notwithstanding its critical stance on gene patenting, the SRT Project was invited by EPO to be one of its expert advisors on future ethical and social issues. It seems clear that present intellectual property regimes will need some radical changes in response to an array of ongoing social changes. One part of the study states:

> Consumers are demanding cheap or even free access to patented or copyright-protected goods. Patient groups have been pressuring governments over the use of costly patented medicines. Scientists are

fighting patents that they feel are blocking research. Programmers are pushing open source projects as an alternative to the established models of IP ownership in the software industry . . . The public at large may be less happy with the idea that incremental change, strategic patents or rights over common knowledge should be profitable for the few.[23]

Thus it seems that some in the patenting world have realized that the ethical and social dimension may perhaps be a vital key to its future.

Suggested further reading

D. Bruce and A. Bruce (eds), *Engineering Genesis*, Earthscan, 1998, ch. 8.

Audrey R. Chapman, *Unprecedented Choices: Religious Ethics at the Frontiers of Genetic Science*, Fortress Press, 1999, ch. 4.

Church of Scotland, *Ethical Concerns about Patenting in Relation to Living Organisms*, Reports of the Church of Scotland General Assembly, Edinburgh, 22 May 1997.

Carlos M. Correa, Traditional Knowledge and Intellectual Property: A Discussion Paper, Quaker Peace and Service, 2001.

European Ecumenical Commission for Church and Society, Submission to the European Parliament on the 'Common Position' of the Draft Directive on the Patenting of Biotechnological Inventions, EECCS, Strasbourg, 28 March 1998.

Geoff Tansey, *Trade, Intellectual Property, Food and Biodiversity: Key Issues and Options for the 1999 Review of Article 27.3(b) of the TRIPS Agreement*, Quaker Peace and Service, 1999.

Two articles in the same journal, giving differing Christian views:

D. M. Bruce, 'Patenting human genes: a Christian view', *Bulletin of Medical Ethics*, January 1997, pp. 18–20.

M. J. Reiss, 'Is it right to patent DNA?', *Bulletin of Medical Ethics*, January 1997, pp. 21–4.

8

The Church and the genomic project to secure the human future

Michael S. Northcott

> Consider God's handiwork: who can straighten what he has made crooked?
>
> Ecclesiastes 7.13 (Revised English Bible)

The film *Gattaca*, whose opening frame displays these words from the book of Ecclesiastes, portrays a vision of a society in which there are two kinds of people: those born with the aid of laboratory science, and those born by 'natural reproduction'.[1] The first are people who have been fertilized *in vitro* by clinicians. Clinicians, in consultation with parents, select individuals at the embryonic stage that conform to genetic traits desired by parents and lack genes indicating a likelihood of developing a range of illnesses including cancers, heart disease and psychological disorders before implantation of the embryo into the womb of the mother. Parents are given a genetic printout of their future child which indicates such details as their height, colour of hair and eyes, and their likely longevity. The second are born of illicit sexual acts between individuals who either choose to have children by 'natural' methods or else simply fail to take contraceptive precautions in the course of sexual intercourse. That in the second case it is necessary to put the word 'natural' in inverted commas already indicates the problem we shall explore in this chapter. What does humanity look like in an era in which it becomes possible through *in vitro* fertilization and manipulation of the human genome to select out certain genetic traits before birth?[2]

In *Gattaca* as in many dystopic science fiction texts the answer is plain.[3] A world in which commercial science controls the human genome is a totalitarian world of technocratic rule in which true human freedom is erased.

Those whose parents' sexual mores or moral beliefs mean that they are born as a race of natural-born outsiders are relegated in the film to a slave or service class who are excluded from elite professions or managerial and technocratic roles. The plot of the film focuses on one such individual who seeks to attain legitimate status and so become an astronaut. In order to achieve this status he has to survive an extraordinary range of regular and invasive biometric tests. To pass these tests he has to carry samples of urine, blood and hair from a legitimate individual who participates in an identity-substitution project. The project runs the risk, however, of falling foul of extensive surveillance technologies which, for example, allow the glasses used at a reception or hairs left on an office carpet to be screened by machines which can identify individuals in a computerized DNA database of the population, both legitimate and illegitimate.

'Perfect love casts out fear' (1 John 4.18)

The potential of the Human Genome Project to advance the kind of society described by *Gattaca*, where genetically cleaned-up individuals represent a master race and others a class of genetic illegitimates, depends on techniques for reading and isolating genetic information which genetic scientists have developed. It also depends on the presence of social conditions in which such techniques are systematically applied to individuals and to classes of individuals for purposes of genetic screening and identity checking by the state and other agencies. And such conditions already exist in the USA, and now in the UK.

The pivotal technique required for assembling a society analogous to that described in *Gattaca* is prenatal genetic screening of embryos and fetuses. As Barbara Rothman observes, prenatal genetic screening for heritable conditions in the USA was associated with race from its inception.[4] Tay-Sachs is a condition which while unobservable at birth leads to an early, lingering and very painful death in infants who have it. Babies progressively lose their hearing, sight and mobility and are ultimately unable to breathe. The condition is associated with Ashkenazi Jews.[5] In Israel and the USA screening of Jewish adults who are planning to conceive began in the 1970s. Adult screening identifies couples who have low levels of an enzyme whose underproduction is the cause of the condition. Both partners must have the condition to be at risk of conceiving children with the disease. Such couples are mostly offered fetal selection through the genetic testing of amniotic fluid. Couples whose fetuses carry the condition are counselled to terminate the pregnancy, and most agree. Pre-implantation genetic diagnosis is used in a smaller number of cases where embryos are fertilized *in vitro* and those that do not have the potential to develop the condition are selected for implantation in the womb. Treatment has been so successful that the condition has been all but eradicated in Israel, while Jewish children born with the disease in the USA are also now rare since most parents choose to abort.

The second most widely available genetic screening programme in the USA is for sickle-cell anaemia. Up to one in ten African Americans carry this disease, which has the advantage that it gives the carrier resistance to malaria, hence its prevalence in Africa. Sickle-cell is, however, unlike Tay-Sachs as its carriers can lead normal lives and achieve old age. Others at varying points in their lives experience acute pains in their limbs that can last for hours or days and may ultimately lead to early death. The US government began a nationwide programme of screening for the disease. However, far fewer resources were devoted to the programme relative to the numbers being screened and counselling was rarely available. The screening programme led to the abortion of many black children. It also led to adults identified as carriers being discriminated against by US government agencies, including the armed forces, and by health insurers. As Barbara Rothman comments, the screening programme was a disaster for black people as it resulted in widespread genetic, and hence racial, discrimination against them.[6]

The first societal use in Britain of genetic fingerprinting also has significant racial overtones. In 1988 scientists at Leicester University were contracted by an immigration lawyer to perform DNA fingerprinting on a Ghanaian boy who had been refused residency by the Home Office on the grounds that his maternity was not as his UK-domiciled mother claimed.[7] DNA evidence 'proved' the claimed maternity and the boy was granted leave to stay. And the use of genetic fingerprinting in relation to the policing of immigration is significantly enhanced by the growing use of such techniques in relation to border security and crime prevention.

The second requirement for the development of a society analogous to that described in *Gattaca* is the adoption of biometric identification techniques for codifying and identifying national populations. And the adoption in Britain and America of a nationwide strategic response to the terrorist attack on the USA in 2001, which governments in both domains have called a 'war on terror', has led to the deployment of a range of new biometric and photographic surveillance techniques on citizens.[8] These techniques had already emerged in the context of the emergent technologization of policing since 1945. The UK police have a large and growing national DNA database of more than five million individuals living in or visiting the UK. Although in principle the database is restricted to anyone who has been charged – though not convicted – of a criminal act, the database also includes DNA samples of rape victims, of illegal immigrants, of demonstrators arrested under public order offences, and even of children of those charged with crimes.[9] Techniques already exist for DNA scanning of hair, saliva, sweat or semen. These techniques are regularly used in forensic crime laboratories and moreover they are used in court to determine the presence or absence of particular individuals at crime scenes. Police are also storing digital images of faces using mass recording of public gatherings such as demonstrations and football matches, which can be digitally searched and accessed. Facial recognition software is combined with such digital images to enable police to monitor crowds to search for particular individuals.

The British government in response to what it sees as a growing terrorist threat has now sought to find ways to extend these screening techniques to the whole populace, and to all individuals who seek to enter the UK, and pass through the growing armoury of biometric and identity checks deployed by the new UK Border Agency. Hence the UK government has put legislation on the statute books setting in train a new citizen identity database that will include information such as fingerprint scans and other unspecified biometric information.[10] This new computer database will moreover be accessible by a range of government and commercial organizations including insurance companies and employers, since part of the declared purpose of the database, according to the Identity Cards Act, is to permit screening for illegal immigrants. Employers will even have a legal duty to screen all new employees using the database under the act.

The scientific patenting and technological manipulation of the human genome which is presently underway in a range of laboratories around the world represents a further and essential element in the assembly of techniques required for the construction of a social world not unlike that presented in *Gattaca*. The identification by scientists in the Human Genome Project of genes which act as markers for particular heritable conditions which have a genetic component will make possible new kinds of genetic discrimination. It also opens up the possibility of the genetic homogenization of the human genome as scientists offer parents the possibility of screening out not only children with Down's syndrome, Tay-Sachs or sickle-cell, but children who may be said to have genes that will render them prone to alcoholism, breast cancer or even depression.

Some may suggest that this degree of genetic screening is not a necessary outcome of the Human Genome Project. But this is to neglect the technological imperative according to which, once it is possible to do something, it gradually becomes acceptable to do it. And as with predecessor technologies such as the splitting of the atom, or the jet engine, the inventors pass to others responsibility for the moral problems involved in the dubious uses to which their inventions may be put.[11]

There are those who suggest that growing technological mastery over nature requires an enhanced human capacity for responsibility and a new ethic of responsibility, and that classical or Christian traditions are incapable of providing this.[12] However, classical and Christian moral traditions give greater moral authority to the forms in which the given order of the world presents itself to humanity. Christians call these 'created order', Greeks 'natural order'. Both suggest that humility and reverence for these forms are crucial if hubristic and ultimately destructive manipulations of nature are to be avoided.[13] At the heart of the moral problem of the modern domination of nature is that it seems to confer on modern industrial humans capacities to control and shape the evolution of species and even the climate of the planet, and not just the human genome, while industrial humans display less responsibility and wisdom in their uses of the planet than any predecessor human civilization.[14] Human genomics advances this in spades. As Michael Sandel suggests, embryo pre-selection and genetic fetal screening increase parental choice such that 'responsibility expands to daunting proportions'.[15] And as choice takes over from chance, control and not destiny becomes the lodestar.

'For those who want to save their life will lose it, and those who lose their life for my sake will save it' (Luke 9.24)

The film *Gattaca*, like other science fiction representations of the 'posthuman' future, such as *Bladerunner* and *AI*, presents a dark and fearful vision of the future. But this dark vision arises from the trajectory represented by present efforts to subject human nature – and nature in general – to technological control in the bid to erase suffering and illness from society and to promote human dominion and progress. As Daniel Callahan suggests, there is something pathological in the desire expressed in modern medicine to extend technological control over the mortal conditions of human life. There is a reason we call someone who attempts to control every aspect of their lives, and sometimes of their colleagues' or relatives' lives, a 'control freak'. There is something morally problematic, and indeed 'out of control', about this desire for control.[16] By increasing power over nature the quest for technological control also increases human powers over other humans, and ultimately therefore the capacity of humans to dehumanize and enslave one another in systems of corporate control, economic management and surveillance where accountability and moral responsibility of particular agents is lost in the diffusion of political sovereignty in 'the system', 'the federation' or 'the borg'.[17]

The extent of the control freakery advanced by genomics is indicated in the claim of President Clinton in 1996 that the Human Genome Project would

> in the not too distant future enable every set of parents that has a little baby to get a map of the genetic structure of their child. So if their child has a genetic predisposition to a certain kind of problem, or even heart disease or stroke in the early 40s, they will be able to plan that child's life, that child's upbringing, to minimize the possibility of that child developing that illness or that predisposition, to organize the diet plan, the exercise plan, the medical treatment, that would enable untold numbers of people to have far more full lives than would have been the case before.[18]

While this futuristic claim for the Human Genome Project is clearly hyperbolic it nonetheless displays an extraordinary openness to the metaphor of control. And it indicates that some do envisage that such detailed predictive knowledge of a child's life prospects – again as also envisaged in *Gattaca* – may become available to clinicians and parents through genetic screening. The question is what such knowledge does to the experience of being parents, and children. As Rothman suggests, such knowledge for parents is more incapacitating than it is empowering. There are limits to how much parents can control their children's lives. And it is not only child-rearing that is potentially infected.

The power that genetic knowledge gives parents and clinicians to control reproductive outcomes is already altering the human experience of conception, and of what it is to *be* a child, in profound ways.[19] Rothman points up the losses in relation to the experience of pregnancy for those involved in genetic screening programmes. If through genetic screening a mother learns that the child she is carrying will die at or very soon after birth she will normally be counselled to terminate the pregnancy. However, mothers and midwives interviewed by Rothman indicate that such decisions often lead to considerable unhappiness in the mother. If the knowledge had not been given to them they would have had the opportunity of experiencing a 'good pregnancy', of carrying a kicking, living being inside them for nine months, and of meeting and grieving the child as body and soul in the few hours, days or weeks of its albeit diminished life. And the decision to terminate on the basis of an assessment of quality of life, or length of life, is also highly ambiguous in another sense. How long must a life *be* before it is worth living?

The clinician views pregnancy as a health condition whose end is the birth of a genetically sound individual. But for the midwives and mothers Rothman interviews, pregnancy – life bearing – is an intrinsic good. For many of them, life, even genetically imperfect life, is also an intrinsic good. The problem, as Sandel suggests, is that the quest for perfection, and the control over human reproduction this quest advances, subverts other vital aspects of the human good which are intrinsic to natality and to life.[20]

The extent of societal investment in attempts to prevent disability and heritable illness by manipulating the genome also holds out the prospect of a society in which there will be fewer and fewer people born with disability. Will such a society be more or less tolerant, more or less just, in the ways in which it cares for and attributes resources to such individuals?

The genomic quest for control over human mortality and natality is indicative of a loss of trust in the biological situatedness of mortal life. Part of this loss of trust issues from the modern liberal narrative of autonomy according to which each individual person is her own creator, responsible for her own fate and flourishing. Thus Ronald Dworkin suggests that ethical individualism requires that individuals 'play God' with their and their children's genes in order to improve their lives.[21] But predecessor cultures which placed a higher value on theonomy – the divine derivation of the laws that give order to the cosmos and human life – than autonomy regarded mortality and natality as features of a set of created, historical and natural givens which the individual was unwise to challenge.[22] Jewish and Christian texts express this sense of value for the created character of human life in terms of blessing, gift and grace and propose that the appropriate creaturely response is one of gratitude and praise.

The conception of life as a gift that is received by the subjects of life from a beneficent creator resists the instrumental manipulation of the human genome in a way that secular liberal conceptions of life – as possession, property or resource – do not. It also provides significant resources for imagining forms of the common good and social solidarity in mortality and natality that enhanced control and discrimination in relation to human genetic inheritance threaten to diminish. This is because the conception of life as a gift suggests that life is received from a higher power. That life is so received indicates the wisdom of humility in receiving life from above or beyond. And this humility suggests a certain reverence for the natural conditions in which life is received.

This reverence suggests openness to surprises that the desire for mastery and control eschews. Liberals seem to dislike surprise as much as they dislike fate. If life – for example the birth of a daughter and not a son, or of a child who wants to be a plumber and not a doctor – can surprise us in the newness of its natality then this suggests that humans are not their own creators. And if they do not make themselves, then this implies that they are not autonomous and free to determine their destinies or ends. Being open to surprises, as Stanley Hauerwas suggests, is about being open to providence, and to the reality that we are not in control, despite all the efforts of modern culture to teach us that we are:

> To live out of control as Christians means that we do not assume that our task as Christians is to make history come out right . . . those who are without control have fewer illusions about what makes this world secure or safe: and they inherently distrust those who say they are going to help through power or violence.[23]

One of the paradoxes of the dystopic visions of the genetically controlled futures presented by science fiction is that they present worlds which are more controlled, more divided *and* more violent, than our own. As Hauerwas suggests, the quest for control does not make us more peaceable or more just. On the contrary, it advances the possibility that we can secure our future, or the future of our children, while leaving behind, shutting out and ultimately defending ourselves against those whom nature or nurture have ill-favoured.

'You received without payment; give without payment' (Matthew 10.8)

At the heart of the Christian vision of peace is the idea that Christians are reconciled to one another by the cross and so made members of the organic and mystical body of Christ which is the Church. Back of this idea of incorporation is that membership of the Church is an unmerited free gift and a divine calling. Modern liberal political theory by contrast envisages social belonging in terms of individual entitlement and choice. The liberal idea of the autonomous individual choosing to join with other individuals for certain purposes does away with the traditional organic model of the body politic. And yet the liberal social contract perspective hardly does justice to the human experience of the social as a field of organic relations. Individuals are born into particular cultures and societies in which they acquire language and entitlements through biological networks of kin relations. However, it is the liberal model of the autonomous individual rather than the organic social which is valorized by the metaphor of genetics as the driver of human identity and health or ill health. And the same holds true for the social vision of human health and well-being advanced by genomics. While some particular genetic conditions have been targeted, more or less successfully, by genetic screening techniques, geneticists are endeavouring to identify marker genes for a whole range of illnesses, including cancers, heart disease and even such conditions as alcoholism, depression and obesity. If it can be said that such conditions are indicated by a person's genes then the metaphor of genetic illness indicates that the individual is responsible, holds in her own skin the causes of her illness. And yet many of the illnesses that are now being recast in this genetic frame are intrinsically more environmental and social than they are heritable and genetic. Cancers are associated with industrial chemicals, with diets high in animal fats and meat, and lifestyles low in exercise. Such chemicals, diets and lifestyles are prevalent in most industrial societies. When geneticists expend great resources seeking to track genes that may mark individuals who get cancer from others who do not, they promote a voluntarist and individualistic metaphor of disease as emanating from genetic information residing in an individual's DNA. They also distract policy makers and public health authorities from addressing the environmental and societal causes of such diseases. As Rothman puts it, it is rather as if the Victorians had told individuals who got cholera to wash their hands more often instead of creating public water supplies and building sewers.[24]

The genetic model has another and equally troubling implication. If individuals are responsible – along with their parents – for the illnesses that they are 'born' with, then the idea of a shared responsibility for conditions such as cancer, and for health in general, disappears. The metaphor of genomic illness therefore promotes the kind of society in which there is no shared health insurance and where access to health is an entitlement for the genetically responsible.
Here we see the grave political dangers implicit in the voluntarist rejection of the organic nature of social being. The embrace of the idea that individuals 'make themselves' also promotes the voluntarist notion of parenting such that the choices of parents and clinicians at or after conception *make* the children who will eventually make themselves as adults. This conception of self-making destroys a sense of social solidarity because by undoing the traditional belief that life is a gift it also subverts the idea that those whose life chances give them more health or more abilities or more wealth ought to share their good fortune

with the less fortunate. If chance in conception is eventually eradicated by the extension of embryo pre-selection and selective abortion to more and more health conditions, then there is no fortune and the unwell become, as they are in *Gattaca*, the undeserving.

'From one to whom much has been entrusted, even more will be demanded' (Luke 12.48b)

The narrative that men and women make themselves in genetic terms, as advanced by the Human Genomic Project, has arisen in the context of a significant cultural shift in Britain and America in the last 40 years. After the Second World War, income inequalities shrank in both countries while public authorities invested heavily in public health, welfare and education programmes in the belief that social mobility was a public good and extreme inequality was harmful to all. However, under the neoliberal economics of Reagan and Thatcher, and as encapsulated in Margaret Thatcher's claim that 'there is no such thing as society', both countries have seen dramatic reductions in social mobility and sharp increases in inequality as measured in terms not only of income but of health outcomes and educational attainment as between rich and poor.

More than 50 million people in the USA have no access to proper health care, and infant mortality rates are no better than those in some of the poorest developing countries. The country that has invested more than any other in genetic screening and genetic therapies is at the same time a country where the wealthy healthy increasingly refuse to recognize that the poor and ill have a claim on them or their taxes. *Gattaca* is of course an American film. For many Americans the condition of health discrimination that it takes to a futuristic extreme is already a reality. And as genetic screening advances, the availability and affordability of health insurance is increasingly tied to the wellness or otherwise to which a person's familial or even racial genetic profile attests.

Christians do well to recall at this point the origins of health care in the Christian narrative of the dying and rising God who healed creation through compassionate service and submission to the conditions of organic and sinful life. The story of the crucified God is of a God who bears creation in Godself and who rebirths creation not by resisting the way of the cross but by going that way. And this story, which ends in the victory of the Risen Lord over the powers that misdirect human life, trains Christians that they too are called to heal the world by a willingness to serve and even to suffer. And it was this narrative that trained Christians to open hostels for the sick and the homeless in imperial Roman cities, and to provide hospitals to pilgrims on the pilgrim paths of medieval Europe. It was in such practices that the Christian practice of health care was born. Shorn of the narrative of the God who heals through service and suffering with God's creatures, health care in the future runs the risk of turning into a selection process whose principal aim is to exclude the suffering rather than to care for them.

The Christian vision of the future is different from the modern belief in technological progress. Those who suggest that modernization and revolution are the way to the future and the past is dead and gone have no conception of the way in which the death and Resurrection of Jesus Christ already represents the destiny of humanity and of all creation. The New Testament writers find in these events all the progress to which humanity can ever aspire, for in them they see the birth of a 'new heaven and a new earth' in which suffering is at an end and God wipes away every tear from the eye. Christians live in the gap between the known past and the known future. And of course this gap is a place of uncertainty where the near future is less well known than the final destiny. But the final destiny, and the apocalyptic events which set the world and humanity toward that destiny, act as a control, a guide, a teleological orientation to human aspirations and human actions in the 'time between the times'. They train Christians that human attempts to grasp control of history and to manage history's outcome – whether for power or wealth or war – are evidence of creaturely hubris, and of a refusal to acknowledge divine power and sovereignty in the revelation of Jesus Christ as Lord of the cosmos in whom all life, all things are held together.[25] They also train Christians that those who claim to redeem humanity from finitude, frailty and mortality represent the principle of antichrist – they promise a way of redemption which denies the way of the cross. And this denial frequently involves imposing suffering and sacrifice on the poor and the suffering and the weak in the present so that some favoured group of humans can enjoy the perfected vision of the future offered by the messianic political leader of corporate entity.

The way of the cross was redemptive because it revealed that God works to redeem the world not in power but in weakness, not in assertions of superiority to creaturely conditions but in subjection to them; the way to redemption turns out to be *through* mortality, through creatureliness, not in rising above creatureliness. The Resurrection of Christ from the dead represents therefore a vindication of created order, and bodily life. Christ's body is the new being within creation, of which there can be no more perfect exemplar. No cleaned-up embryo can be as perfect as the risen body of Christ. And the body of Christ is the physical and ontological foundation for the Church. Christians are united by the story of Christ's life, death and Resurrection. The memory of these events is paradigmatic for the hopes and actions of Christians. But Christians are also united in the body of Christ as they participate in eucharistic worship in which their individual identities become one with his mortal body and with one another in a communal realization of the perfected humanity which is the destiny of all human beings as the 'new creation'. The Christian hope for redeeming the human condition in this life from injustice and suffering is intricately connected with the politics of the body of Christ in which the weak are given a voice alongside the strong, and all are united in their common subjection to the headship of Christ. And this hope trains Christians that there are no utopias, no future states – other than the new heaven and the new earth – in which frail bodies, mortality and suffering will not also be present.

The particular concern Christians have with the relief of suffering and sickness is therefore not just about the end goal of healing, for some will not be healed, and in one sense none will be healed, apart from the supreme healing of the human condition which is the resurrected body of Christ. The focus is rather on the way in which humans care for one another and heal one another in the midst of suffering.

It is no coincidence then that the first hospitals were hostels for the poor and the sick attached to bishops' houses in fourth-century Mediterranean cities, and later to the houses of monastic orders. Health care – and after all it is health care in which genomics is socially situated – in the Christian West originates as a way of mimicking who God was revealed to be in Christ. It was the acting out of the body of Christ in a suffering world. Similarly, it is no coincidence that the genomics project arises at a time when health care is increasingly being subjected to mathematical formulae and the accountant's rule. Markets and targets and cost-benefit analysis are imposed on health-care institutions not because they reduce costs. Far from it; the costs of administration have quadrupled in the UK in the last 15 years. Rather it is because of the modern faith in the certainty of outcomes that numbers seem to represent. Neoliberalism is remodelling society after the physics of the nineteenth century on which neoclassical economics itself was modelled. This pre-Einsteinian physics seemed to define certain fixed laws which explained the relationships of all bodies in the universe without reference to a creator or to mystery. The attempt to subject every area of human life including childcare and health care, education and even religion to the market is an outgrowth of the mistaken cosmology of mechanism in the twenty-first century, and its hubristic quest for certainty and control.

But on the approach outlined above health care is not reducible to mathematical targets or estimates of effectiveness. It is instead about process, quality of care, relationships between poor and rich, sick and well, patient and clinician. These things are in principle not measurable by the accountant's rule, nor reducible to calculations of profit by a health-care corporation.

This has tremendous significance for thinking about the patenting of the human genome and the larger genomics project. The project represents the attempt by scientists and technocrats to reduce the mortal conditions of finitude to a mathematical code which is manipulable and perfectible. The ends in view are to clean up the genome, to identify genes associated with particular illnesses and to offer genetic therapies for existing conditions. But the economic resources devoted to this project by the most 'advanced' countries have been garnered by these countries at the cost of more than two hundred years of imperial exploitation of colonial domains and of an ecological footprint that continues to overshadow and subjugate the lives of the 'unadvanced' or the 'underdeveloped', who include more than one-fifth of humanity. The diseases which blight the lives of the poor include malaria, tuberculosis and diarrhoea. The incidence of all of these diseases is actually rising and this is the case even among some communities in the advanced countries as the constant global exchange of people sees rates of TB growing even in the northern hemisphere.

Genetic discrimination will only advance these kinds of existing enforced economic bargains in which some are excluded from the insurable good life promised by cleaned up germ-line and genetic therapies because of their country of origin or even their manner of birth. But the point is, of course, that the genomics project itself already rests upon a kind of genetic discrimination for, like the eugenics project of the 1920s and 1930s, its priorities are the genetic conditions and affluence diseases of rich, mostly white people and not the much more common conditions of the unprivileged or non-white.

Scientists often refuse to acknowledge that their findings are in any way determined by social context or faith systems outside of the frame of data analysis and empirical validation and falsification. However, the turn to genomics as the ultimate therapeutic tool has not arisen in a cultural and ideological vacuum. The present turn to the procedures of mathematical discrimination and markets, rather than participative political procedures, to govern social life is already advancing atomization and inequality, and undermining a sense of solidarity and commitment to the common good of humanity in those societies – Britain and the USA – which have most fully embraced this new form of governance by numbers. It is also leading already to a loss of trust in politicians, who increasingly resign their ability to determine the outcomes of economic procedures to autonomous processes. On this analogy the turn of medicine to the same kind of expert management of genetic information is likely to have analogous results. The resulting loss of trust in clinicians, and in the larger health-care business, may likely produce more harms than the benefits putatively held out by therapeutics derived from genomic information.

Virtue in health care arises in significant ways from relationships between carers and patients, and from the shared story of care in which both participate. The reductionism of genetic therapies, combined with the commercial interests which increasingly drive this expensive work forward, is likely to lead to a loss of virtue in clinician–patient relations as commercial drivers, patented knowledge and mathematical estimates of clinical effectiveness of competing procedures among competing providers and potential patients take the place of relational medicine.

In the narrative of health care sustained by Christians health care is intricately connected with the form of the body of Christ, which answers in a unique and definitive way the human longing for community which is ordered not by disordered desires for power or profit but by love for the highest good, which is God. Trust and solidarity are intricately connected to the capacity of faith groups – and of Christian churches in particular – to elicit shared commitment to the supreme object of love, who is God. The paradox of capitalism and commodification is that contractual relationships freeride on what economists sometimes call 'social capital' in which religious communities are notably rich. But the corporate freerider does not just ride for free. The economic corporation contests with the ecclesiological corporation for the soul of the believer and for the collective faith of the community. The more individuals commit to corporate goals of profit maximization and are subjected to the depoliticized procedures of quantitative economic management, the more these goals and procedures infect and subvert the virtues of religious community.

9

A methodological interlude: a case for *rapprochement* between moral theology and moral philosophy

Nigel Biggar

Moral theology and moral philosophy tend not to understand each other very well – to their mutual detriment, and at the expense of public deliberation. Alerted by Karl Barth and reminded by Stanley Hauerwas, much contemporary moral theology – and not just in Protestant circles – is concerned about its Christian theological identity. This concern is perfectly proper in so far as it aspires to display a vision of moral life that is consistent with theological presuppositions. What is there to object to – indeed, what is not to admire – in the desire for intellectual integrity?

The issue, however, is not simply one of consistency. It is also one of theological comprehensiveness. There are some theologians who suppose that the doctrine of creation authorizes 'autonomous' ethics. That is, they believe that a sufficient account of the good and the right can be constructed out of what is universally given in human 'nature' (including the nature of human practical reason), and without appeal to anything revealed in the biblical tradition and par excellence in the nature, life, death and Resurrection of Jesus. At most, the Bible and the 'Christ-event' confirm what 'reason', deep down, knows already. There is nothing inconsistent about this view: it can give a coherent account of how theology does, and does not, relate to ethics. But for those theologians who are concerned about the Christian theological identity of Christian ethics, it is not adequate. It is not adequate, because it is theologically undernourished. What biblical tradition and the Christ-event reveal about the nature of God and the human situation does more than merely rubber-stamp what 'reason' knows anyway (so long as it thinks straight). They modify in important ways how we perceive what is good and right. For example, it is at least controversial whether or not 'nature' or 'reason' recognizes that right relationship with God is a human good – that is, belongs to the flourishing of human beings.[1] The story of Jesus and its biblical hinterland, however, are in no doubt that it does. Again, whether one conceives the special value of human beings as consisting in their capacity for rationality, or in their capacity for responsibility before God, makes a difference to which instances of human being get included in the class of valuable ones. Rationality, as the moral philosopher James Rachels conceives it, limits worthwhile human life – and worthwhile human lives – to those that are capable of planning and executing a 'biography'. Responsibility as the capacity to appreciate given, created goods, on the other hand, extends the boundaries of the class of worthwhile human lives to include that of the autistic child who, though hardly capable of constructing a 'biography', lights up her face at the sound of music.[2] Further still, in the eyes of some conceptions of 'nature' or 'reason' – say, those of Thomas Hobbes – it is not rational (in the sense of prudent) to sacrifice one's life for the sake of truth or justice. In the light of the Christian biblical story, however, self-sacrifice is saved from imprudence and irrationality by the hope that springs from the Resurrection of Jesus from the dead. The biblical theological tradition, and the Christ-event in particular, do indeed make a difference at certain points to what should be considered good and right; and the concern that ethics should be appropriately shaped by what has been revealed through *history*, as well as through 'nature' or 'reason', seems to me quite correct.

Sometimes, however, the healthy concern for the theological integrity of ethics degenerates into a neurotic one for distinctiveness. Here the desire is not so much for comprehensive consistency as it is for *difference*. This strikes me as being quite beside the point. Whether and where and how far a Christian ethic is distinctive depends on what it is being compared with, and what it is being compared about. If the Christian ethicist is sitting on a medical ethics committee composed entirely of various kinds of (Kantian) humanist – agnostic, atheist and religious – and if the topic is that of the genetic engineering of human beings, then much of what his own theological views lead him to say about human dignity and equality and freedom will find echo in the contributions of others. If, on the other hand, he finds himself in the company of Utilitarians and Nietzscheans, then he will find that what he has to say begins to sound rather more distinctive. Similarly, on the issue of the ethics of genetic engineering the moral theologian might well share with his non-religious humanist colleagues a concern to protect embryonic human individuals from having their embryonic beings and their subsequent lives predetermined in important respects by self-regarding and domineering others. However, with regard to the legalization of physician-assisted suicide or voluntary euthanasia, he might find that his belief in human sinfulness makes him considerably more pessimistic (or less complacent) than other humanists when it comes to guesstimating the long-term impact on social common sense of permitting intentional medical killing (under whatever restrictions) to become normal practice.[3] The phenomenon of an overlapping consensus therefore does not imply that theology is irrelevant to deciding what is good and right, and that theologians can simply rely on a common moral sense or natural 'reason' when discussing such things with non-Christians.[4] The phenomenon is contingent. In certain circumstances, in certain company, and on certain topics theology will make no ethical difference. But in other circumstances, in different company, and on other topics, it will. But whether or not the utterances of moral theology are distinctive should be of no concern whatsoever to the moral theologian. What matters is that moral theology should take due account of the full range of theological topics that are relevant to the ethical matter in hand. What matters is integrity, not distinctiveness. The happy fact that others agree should not be taken as a sign that moral theology has somehow failed to be true to itself. If the moral theologian is true to the doctrine of creation, then he should expect to find some agreement: Christians and non-Christians are, after all, fellow creatures in a single, universally given moral world. And if his pneumatology allows that the Spirit of God-in-Christ makes himself known beyond the bounds of visible, institutional churches; and if his ecclesiology allows that the Spirit of God-in-Christ wins acceptance from some who, for reasons of historical or cultural or biographical accident, have not yet identified the Spirit of God with the Jesus of the Christian Churches' confession, then the theologian may even expect the extent of overlapping consensus with non-Christians (or anonymous ones) to exceed that which reflection on 'nature' or 'reason' strictly permits.

If much moral theology is anxiously concerned to assert its distinctiveness, much moral philosophy is content to ignore theology – or, if not to ignore it, then to misrepresent it. As witness I call the political philosopher, Jeremy Waldron:

> Secular theorists often assume that they know what a religious
> argument is like: they present it as a crude prescription from God,
> backed up with the threat of hellfire, derived from general or particular
> revelation, and they contrast it with the elegant simplicity of a
> philosophical argument by Rawls (say) or Dworkin. With this image in

mind, they think it obvious that religious argument should be excluded from public life . . . But those who have bothered to make themselves familiar with existing religious-based arguments in modern political theory know that this is mostly a travesty . . .[5]

From a theological point of view this philosophical neglect could be charitably ascribed to the correct assumption that all human beings inhabit a single moral universe, and that much ethical mileage can be made simply by reference to 'nature' and 'reason'. However, the truth is that most contemporary philosophical neglect of moral theology can be laid at the feet of doctrinaire atheist conviction. It has simply been assumed that religion is inexorably on the wane, that theology is puerile nonsense and that religious traditions could not have anything interesting and true to say about ethical matters. This has meant, not only that theological elements in the canon of moral philosophy have been suppressed[6], but that moral theology has been alienated from an implicitly – sometimes explicitly – atheist moral philosophy. The resultant combination of moral theology's anxious concern with its own distinctiveness, and moral philosophy's arrogant assumption that theology isn't worth listening to, serves to confirm the conviction that public discussion of ethical matters must be 'secular' in the sense of 'secularist' or 'non-religious'. Theology is arcane and inaccessible to 'us' – that is, right-thinking, rational, modern people. Public discussion of ethical issues, then, must be conducted in the 'neutral' language of philosophy.

There are a number of problems with this situation. First, theologians who are keen on being distinctively Christian *theologians* are sometimes wont to restrict their brief to the explication of the ethical import of theological concepts – and to leave to others the task of applying the resultant theological ethic in the various spheres of human life. Karl Barth, for example, distinguished between 'theological ethics' and its practical application in 'Christian ethics', and confined himself to the former.[7] A charitable view could consider this division of labour as reasonable, in so far as it is surely true that no one can do everything. After all, Barth himself spent the best part of 40 years writing his *Church Dogmatics* – which included a comprehensive theological ethic – and he *still* didn't complete it. On the other hand, if the moral theologian is not willing to work out his theological ethic right down to ground level, then who does he imagine will do it for him? Moreover, this thorough working out is not merely a matter of the technical 'application' of ready-made, idiot-proof instructions. Rather, it is a dialectical process of interpretation, whereby the meaning of theological ethical concepts is developed, modified and even revised in the course of bringing them to bear on fields of human life and concrete situations. For this reason I think it fair to say that a theological ethic that hasn't worked its way thoroughly through a variety of moral cases can have, at best, only a vague and unrefined grasp of what it's talking about.

Some moral theologians don't go far enough. Others, however, go too far, too fast. They venture judgements without ethics. What I mean by this is that they attempt to settle moral matters by direct appeal to theological categories, without availing themselves of non-theological ethical concepts,[8] and bypassing relevant moral philosophical discussions. The result is either an indeterminate and ineffectual conclusion, or one whose connection with its premises is hard to discern. So, for one example, some moral theologians have sought to pronounce on the morality of legalizing voluntary euthanasia without having bothered first to negotiate and take a position in the tricky philosophical debate about whether or not it makes sense to distinguish between an intended death and one that is foreseen but unintended. The debate might be an old one; but it remains nonetheless crucial. For another example, to protest against genetic engineering because it involves 'playing God' or transgressing God-given natural boundaries doesn't explain why *this* intervention is morally wrong, whereas all the other interventions that have become customary in medical practice are OK. One of the most exegetically sound meanings of the biblical notion that human beings have been created 'in the image of God' is that they have been granted the dignity of being God's vicegerents on earth – that is, they have been given the responsibility of managing the rest of creation under God. On the one hand, this implies that human beings are not puppets, but responsible agents with room for discretion and creativity. To be human is to be in the business of innovation. But to be human is also to be responsible to God the creator. When, then, is innovation responsible, and when is it not? How can we distinguish innovation from (sinful) transgression? Or how can we tell the creative transgression of the given from immoral transgression? The answers to these questions, I think, must come in the form of an ethical analysis that operates immediately in terms of justice and prudence (and ultimately in terms of 'natural' or given basic human goods). Too often, however, theologians settle for rhetoric – distinctively theological, reassuringly prophetic, but lacking moral grip.

On the moral philosophical side, the current situation is problematic in two related respects. First, it is unsatisfactory – not to mention unprofessional and illiberal – that moral philosophers should dismiss out of hand religious traditions of ethical discussion, which have achieved not a little refinement and wisdom over many centuries, on the basis of ignorant caricature.[9] Second, philosophers have a habit of talking about what 'we' think ethically. Sometimes this reflects an honest attempt to capture, and think out of, current common moral sense; but all too often it forgets the social limitations of its reach. Too often, on closer inspection, 'we' turn out to be clones of the philosopher: Western, modernist, rationalist and atheist. But this world is not the whole world. It's not even the whole truth. The imperialist, patronizing, doctrinaire 'we' gives no space or voice to non-conformists – among them religious believers. Likewise, philosophers often speak of 'reason' as if it could mean one thing only, and so without further explanation or justification. But, as I have suggested, what's reasonable to an orthodox Christian will not be reasonable to a Hobbesian. What's reasonable bears some thinking about – and talking about with *others*.

Arrogant dismissiveness on the part of moral philosophers, combined with moral theologians' anxious concern for distinctiveness, conspire together to weaken the quality of public deliberation. On the one hand, the theologians are not very skilled at explicating the connections between their theology and their ethics, and so at commending the former to non-believers or half-believers who buy the latter. Nor are they much inclined to show how their theology bears significantly upon non-theological ethical discourse. As a consequence, non-theologians – even those whose scepticism is sympathetic – are left baffled and not at all persuaded that theology has anything interesting to offer. Add to this the doctrinaire dismissiveness of atheist philosophy – fortified in its prejudices by the menacing authoritarianism of religious fundamentalism – and it seems self-evident that public deliberation must proceed in non-religious, secularist terms.

There are several problems with this. One is that it tends to assume that 'we' are all 'secular' – which is to say, virtually atheist. Actually, 'we' are much more various than that. If 'we' refers to the population of the UK – commonly said to be one of Europe's most 'secular' countries – then we comprise minorities of convinced atheists, of religious fundamentalists, of non-fundamentalist religious observants, and a majority of people who are more or less agnostic. The second problem is that it tends to leave the impression that once theology has been banned, public deliberation is then free to proceed in metaphysically neutral, autonomous, universally shared terms that are socially cohering. This is, of course, nonsense. The ethical views of Kantians and Utilitarians and Nietzscheans, of Neoliberals and Socialists and Greens, of Burkeans and Modernizers and Leninists, are not metaphysically free-standing and they are all quite as capable of giving rise to provisionally intractable disagreements as those of Christians and Muslims. A third problem is that it relegates theology to the role of a private recreation – which is a role that much self-respecting theology (Christian, as well as Islamic) cannot, and should not, accept.

That's the situation, and those are the problems. So what's to be done about it? Of course moral theologians should take their theology seriously, but less for the sake of shoring up identity than attesting the truth about what's good and right. Sometimes theology will have something fresh and unusual to say – but not at all levels, and not at every point, and not in every kind of company. Integrity is a moral and intellectual virtue; distinctiveness is merely an ephemeral historical phenomenon. And moral theology should not regard itself necessarily and simply as an *alternative* to moral philosophy. That might be so when moral philosophy bears the imprint of a methodical atheism; but not all moral philosophy is so impressed. Besides, there are philosophical concepts that the moral theologian needs, and philosophical debates that the moral theologian must negotiate and adjudicate, if he is to bring his theology to bear upon concrete cases precisely and persuasively – and if the full ethical import of his theology is to be disclosed.

Moral philosophers, on the other hand, should stop behaving according to an outdated theory of secularization. It now seems that religion is not moribund, even in the modernized world, and that its influence is going to be significant for the foreseeable future. That isn't to say that religion's claims are true, of course; although a cursory review of a representative sample of its proponents would show that, while some are no doubt credulous and superstitious, others are intellectually searching and sophisticated. Nor is it to say that religion's continuing influence will be for the good; although a fair-minded perusal of its history would reveal a mixed record, not a uniformly dismal one. There is evidence that the penny has dropped with some moral philosophers, who are becoming 'post-secularist'. Recent years have yielded at least two instances of unusual respect for religious ethics expressed by eminent moral philosophers, who are themselves not religious believers. (Neither of them, as it happens, is British.) In December 2002 *Le Monde* published an interview with the German philosopher, Jürgen Habermas. The focus of the interview was the ethics of genetic engineering, and in the course of it Habermas paid tribute to religious traditions' 'superior capacity for articulating our moral sensibility', urged 'a respectful approach' to them, and claimed for them 'at least the same right to make themselves heard in public space'.[10] The previous year, again in a context marked by concern about genetic engineering, he claimed that secular society cannot afford to sever itself from the 'important resources of meaning' that religions represent.[11] Similarly in *Democracy and Tradition* the American philosopher, Jeffrey Stout, has argued against those reckoning religion a 'conversation-stopper', that religious believers may plausibly demonstrate their entitlement to theological premises (even though others may still be entitled to refuse them), and that they should be free to express these freely and fully in a dialectical, improvisational public 'conversation' about the common good.[12] Whether these two instances amount to straws in the wind, we wait to see.

If, however, they are symptoms of an incipient general *rapprochement* on the part of moral philosophy toward theology, and if moral theology is able to turn to meet it, then we can look forward to public discussion becoming 'secular', rather than 'secularist'. Instead of banning theology (uniquely) in the name of some spuriously 'neutral' public discourse, 'secular' public discussion would be genuinely plural. It would invite seriously different points of view to negotiate candidly, but responsibly,[13] and to reach provisional agreements about the common good – for example, about laws governing practices of genetic intervention. These agreements would be provisional in so far as they do not embody the whole truth, as every party sees it, and therefore do not preclude ongoing debate and the possibility of future revision. Should public discussion become more 'secular' in this (finitely)[14] open, Augustinian sense, then moral theology could expect to become the stronger for less suspicious and more honest engagement with moral philosophy, be it merely non-theological or actually atheist. The Church, therefore, could expect to find itself better equipped to make contributions to public deliberation that command wide respect for their combination of self-confidence, logical and analytical thoroughness and critical openness. It could also expect to be better able to display why its theology *matters* ethically – that is, why it is important for the humane quality of human and social life. This is no small way to furnish unbelievers or half-believers with reasons to believe.

10

Conclusion: God, the 'whole' person and the human genome

Mark Bratton

Theology should, in principle, have something to say about everything. This follows on logically from the premise that if this is the one God's one world, then nothing can possibly lie beyond the reach of God's steadfast love. This applies as much to the molecular, as it does to the cosmic, dimensions of human existence, for 'all things have been created through him and for him' in whom 'all things hang together' (Colossians 1.16–17). Accordingly, all fields of human endeavour are proper subject matter for theological reflection, in the face of arguments that theology has nothing worthwhile to contribute to public life and should limit itself to mere commentary on matters of 'private' spirituality. Without some notion of 'public' theology, David Sheppard's injunction to shed 'the light of the gospel on the issues of the day' to which Philip Giddings refers in the Foreword would make no sense. A truly public theology necessarily implies interdisciplinary engagement which, at its best, is both illuminating and mutually transformative.

Distinguishing proper engagement from pontification though requires judgement. Perhaps 'prophetic' churlishness is necessary to disperse the utilitarian common sense which characterizes so much ethical debate in the area of biotechnology and to expose the covert metaphysical assumptions on which a great deal of policy making in the area of biotechnology rests. The positivist tradition which appears to drive a great deal of scientific and ethical thinking assumes a clear-eyed view of human motivation and the consequences of one's actions. A great deal of philosophical medical ethics is arguably premised on this kind of epistemological self-confidence. Donald Bruce, Michael Northcott, Peter Manley Scott and Robert Song, however, each draw attention in their respective contributions to the human capacity for self-deception and mistaking the human desire for control and perfectibility for the demands of beneficence. Drawing attention to a culture's obsessions and delusions may sound plangently off-putting to secular philosophers and a 'secular' public, but is no less true and important to articulate for all that.

On the other hand, distinguishing allegedly prophetic insight into the human condition and various forms of alleged irrationalism sometimes associated with Christian theology also requires a judgement call. Acknowledging the intellect's inadequacy to grasp the truth alone does not necessarily validate what is really another form of dubious epistemological self-confidence, in this case, rooted in theology. On this view, taken to an extreme, secular philosophy would represent an intellectual *non sequitur*, having nothing of value to offer theological reflection. This would be a travesty of the long history of robust and fruitful interaction between Christian and non-Christian thought and promote the kind of interdisciplinary illiteracy that could, and sometimes does, give theology and the Church a bad name. Annette Cashmore has reinforced the requirement for a thorough grasp of the scientific issues that pertain to biotechnology as a prerequisite for theological consideration. John Overton, with his 'craft knowledge' of intellectual property law has made crystal clear what a patent is and *isn't*. Even if in the final analysis there are theologically sound objections to human genome patenting, it does the Church no credit to base its objections on a misconstrual of the nature of patents. Sue Chetwynd has demonstrated that grasping philosophical distinctions does matter if theologians and Church members are to be properly discriminating in their judgements about justifiable and unjustifiable behaviour. And Nigel Biggar, in a contribution of particular importance, argues that theology can be 'reasonable', if not immediately accessible, and thus has a public vocation in the market square.

The various contributions to this book, taken as a whole, outline an approach to moral theology in a pluralistic culture, which fully realized would be, as Biggar says elsewhere, characterized by 'a commitment to the truth, humility, a readiness to be taught, patience, carefulness, [and] charity'.[1] The manifestation of these moral and intellectual virtues would represent a principled, but broader-ranging, development of that tradition of Anglican social theology that Malcolm Brown expounds in his Preface to this book.

It is beyond the scope of this Conclusion to offer a detailed view of what and how a theologically robust, but engaging, moral theology might develop in connection with developments in human genome science. However, it is suggested that this method of doing Christian moral theology can equip Christians to address three key, and interrelated, concerns in a secularizing and secularized culture.

Firstly, the ethical and theological issues relating to the human genome are germane to the widespread search for a 'holistic' understanding of the human person. Advances in human genome science have stimulated the question whether human beings are ultimately no more than the sum of their genetic constituents, or whether they are higher than mere nature, aspiring to find fulfilment in communion with a transcendent reality, namely God. As human genomic sciences break down the human person into his or her physical and molecular constituents, there is also an intensifying perception of the complex and interactive character of biological processes. Clinical science has a need to put components back together into functioning systems, requiring a holistic view of function, from molecule to integrated organism. The widespread interest in 'spirituality' within medicine and wider society has been stimulated by the widely shared conviction that human beings are more than merely physical. The biblical insight that human beings are integrated totalities of mind, body and spirit, with ties in nature, society and history, called to realize the image of God within them, provides a sound theological basis not only for the holistic orientation of clinical science, but a concept of well-being which extends beyond the conventional boundaries of medicine.

Secondly, the ethical and theological issues relating to the human genome are relevant to issues of *identity*. Advances in human genome science have stimulated the question whether my personal identity is reducible to my genetic inheritance, or the circumstances within which I was brought into being; or whether my identity is rooted in more fundamental ground, for example the 'image of God' in me, realized in the baptism which faith makes effective. For example, the deliberate selection of a particular kind of embryo for allegedly ulterior purposes, such as in the case of saviour siblings, straddles the boundary line between responsible parenthood and the improper commodification of children. The biblical concern with questions of genetic inheritance, if not the science of genetics, is central to questions of personal, social and religious identity. The New Testament view is that a person's primary identity is his or her baptism. It transcends all material criteria – genetic, ethnic, physical and social – and provides a powerful corrective to forms of genetic reductionism and determinism which seek to assimilate the 'whole' human person to material elements such as genes.

Thirdly, the ethical and theological issues relating to the human genome are pertinent to the quest for *community*. Advances in human genomic science are placing in question the traditional emphasis western ethical and legal culture has placed on notions of personal sovereignty. The rhetoric of individual autonomy which features so strongly in public discourse is under challenge from sharpened awareness of our strong genetic links with those closest to us, and indeed the whole living world. The biblical insight that human beings are constitutively relational beings knitted into webs of relationship, rather than *atomized* individuals, provides the basis for a powerful critique of the contractual styles of thinking that pervade health care, for example the view that patients are essentially consumers of health services. The sharpened awareness of our genetic affiliation with the wider human community is intensifying the importance of the concept of human *solidarity* as an ethical principle of the first order. This has relevance for domestic political ecologies where the creation of genetic 'underclasses' is not simply a figment of a science fiction writer's imagination but the predictable and anticipated result of an unholy marriage between scientific progress and untrammelled commercial logic. It also has relevance for the global political ecology where the disenfranchisement of whole populations from the benefits of the commercial exploitation of shared genetic information gives another dimension to the power imbalance between developed and developing worlds.

In the final analysis, Christian theology unifies and justifies these three universal elements of human desire within the life of the God himself, who, in Jesus Christ, has drawn close to us, and remains close to us through the Holy Spirit. The God who is above and beyond all things, but created all things, has proved his solidarity with us by dwelling among us, dying for our sakes, and rising again in glory, so that in him, we too, and all creation, might be transformed from one level of glory to another (2 Corinthians 3.18). The light of the gospel has been spread abroad in Jesus Christ. The calling of the moral theologian, and the Church moral theologians serve, is to reflect the light of Christ, so that men and women everywhere might see and rejoice.

Glossary

Base: A nitrogenous component of DNA. There are four: adenine (referred to as A), cytosine (C), guanine (G) and thymine (T).

Base pairs: A pair of complementary bases in the DNA that are held together by a hydrogen bond. Adenine is complementary to, and always bonds with, thymine; cytosine bonds with guanine (AT and CG).

Cell: The smallest unit of an organism that displays the characteristics of life. A cell usually comprises an outer limiting membrane enclosing the cytoplasm and a nucleus which contains the chromosomes.

Cell division: The process by which a cell replicates, and through which an organism grows.

Chromosome: A long DNA molecule containing genes in linear sequence, bound together with proteins, and enormously compacted to form a thread-like structure located in the nucleus of a cell. In humans there are 23 pairs of chromosomes, one of each pair being derived from the mother, the other from the father.

Cloning: A process whereby an identical genetic copy is made of a gene, DNA fragment, cell or an individual. Identical twins are natural clones in that they arise from the splitting of a single fertilized egg, and thus start off with the same genetic material.

DNA: Deoxyribonucleic acid (DNA) comprises two polynucleotide chains linked by their complementary bases. It acquires the shape of a double helix and carries genetic information encoded in the order of the bases.

Embryo: The earliest stages of development of an organism. In humans this covers stages after the first cell division of the fertilized egg through to the end of the eighth week when most of the major organs have been formed. Thereafter, it is called a fetus.

Gamete: Ova (eggs) and sperm are called gametes.

Gene: A hereditary unit of DNA that contains encoded genetic information that is transcribed and translated to form a specific polypeptide chain. A gene may vary in length from a few hundred to more than a million bases.

Gene mapping: Determines the specific location of genes on the chromosomes and the position of genes in relation to one another.

Genetic screening: A process of testing whole populations of people at risk of developing a particular (usually genetic) disease, to identify those who actually will develop the condition.

Genome: The entire genetic complement of an organism.

Genomics: The study of all aspects of the entire genome of an organism, including the DNA sequence, and the location, expression and function of the genes, and their interaction.

Human Fertilization and Embryology Authority (HFEA): The independent regulator, established by statute, that oversees the use of gametes and embryos in fertility treatment and research. It licenses centres to perform assisted conception procedures and human embryo research, and approves research projects. It also provides a range of detailed information on these matters, and on the record of each clinic, for patients, professionals and the public.

Human Genome Project (HGP): An international collaborative effort to sequence the entire human genome and identify and locate the genes.

Intellectual Property (IP): An umbrella term for commercially valuable ideas or products of the intellect, including patents, copyright, trade marks and trade secrets.

Molecule: A stable collection of atoms held together by strong chemical bonds comprising the smallest particle of a substance that retains its physical and chemical properties.

Mutation: A change in the genetic material, either the DNA or a chromosome. If this change is carried by a gamete then it is inherited.

Nucleotide: A nucleotide consists of a nitrogenous base (A, C, G or T), a pentose sugar and a phosphate group. Two long chains of nucleotides (polynucleotides), running in opposite directions and linked by their complementary bases, form DNA.

Patent: A form of IP in which an inventor sacrifices trade secrecy in return for a temporary commercial monopoly (usually 20 years) on the exploitation of the invention. The success of a patent application will depend on satisfying a number of well-established legal criteria which are broadly similar in Europe and the USA.

Pharmacogenetics: Describes the study of genetic variation within populations that leads to one individual person having a different response to a drug from another. This is important because adverse reactions to drugs account for more than one in twenty hospital admissions in the West. It also includes the study of genes involved in the metabolism of drugs within the body.

Polymerase chain reaction (PCR): A technique for replicating and amplifying a small piece of DNA chemically in the laboratory. Each newly produced replica is itself then used in further replication so that the process proceeds as a chain reaction in an exponential manner. Many millions of copies of the original piece of DNA can rapidly be produced. PCR is a vital tool in research and in cloning, and in the diagnosis of hereditary diseases, forensics and paternity testing.

Polypeptide chain: A string of amino acids, one or more of which constitutes a protein.

Pre-implantation genetic diagnosis (PGD): A screening process whereby an embryo after fertilization but before implantation, or even an unfertilized egg or sperm, is tested for a particular suspected genetic defect that would predispose the child to a specific health problem. It requires *in vitro* fertilization, but has the advantage that it avoids the need for decisions on pregnancy termination if prenatal diagnosis is performed at a later stage of pregnancy.

Prenatal diagnosis: Testing of an embryo or a fetus to determine whether it has a particular (usually genetic) disease or is at high risk of having it, using several methods: chorionic villus sampling, amniocentesis, fetal blood sampling and ultrasonography.

Proteins: Complex molecules made up of hundreds or thousands of amino acids arranged in one (monomer) or more (polymer) long chains. Proteins contribute to the cellular structure and, as enzymes, carry out most of the chemical reactions that take place in cells and in the body. The amino acid sequence of a protein is encoded in the sequence of bases in its gene.

Recombinant DNA: DNA derived by joining small segments of DNA from two different sources. Such genetic manipulation can be used to investigate gene function, and can also be used to create human therapeutic agents, or 'novel' organisms for research, such as the 'oncomouse', or agriculturally useful crops, such as drought-resistant plants.

Sequencing: The biochemical process of determining the order of nucleotide bases (A, C, G, T) in the DNA, and the order of amino acids in a protein.

Further reading

Understanding genetic science

A beautifully produced and clearly written dictionary of DNA science is J.
L. Witherly, G. P. Perry and D. L. Leja, *An A to Z of DNA Science: What Scientists
Mean When They Talk About Genes and Genomes*, Cold Spring Harbor
Laboratory Press, 2002.

The story of the Human Genome Project

The fascinating story of the Human Genome Project is put into its context
within the history of genetic science in W. Bodmer and R. McKie, *The Book of
Man: The Human Genome Project and the Quest to Discover our Genetic
Heritage*, Oxford University Press, 1994. The science, personalities and politics
of the Human Genome Project are splendidly told by James Shreeve in J.
Shreeve, *The Genome War: How Craig Venter Tried to Capture the Code of Life
and Save the World*, Ballantine Books, 2005. The story is told from the vantage
point of one of the key players in the public consortium behind the genome
effort in J. Sulston and G. Ferry, *The Common Thread: Science, Politics, Ethics
and the Human Genome*, Bantam Press, 2002. The story is also told by one of
the chief architects of the private genome effort in J. Craig Venter, *A Life
Decoded: My Genome: My Life*, Allen Lane, 2007.

Understanding human genome patenting

David Resnik offers a very clear moral analysis of genome patenting in
D. Resnik, *Owning the Genome: A Moral Analysis of DNA Patenting*, State
University of New York Press, 2003.

Sociological and philosophical reflections on the genetic revolution

A marvellously readable, insightful and human reflection upon the impact of the genetic revolution by a social theorist is B. K. Rothman, *Genetic Maps and Human Imaginations: The Limits of Science in Understanding Who We Are*, Norton, 1998. A short, engaging, extremely lucid, and religiously sympathetic, philosophical engagement with developments in biomedical science is M. J. Sandel, *The Case against Perfection: Ethics in the Age of Genetic Engineering*, Belknap Press, 2007.

Theological reflection on advances in human genetics

A fairly comprehensive treatment of the various 'topics' in human genetics can be found in C. Deane-Drummond, *Genetics and Christian Ethics*, Cambridge University Press, 2006, including genetic screening, counselling, therapy and patenting. An interdisciplinary collection of essays on the human genome can be found in C. Deane-Drummond (ed.), *Brave New World: Theology, Ethics and the Human Genome*, Continuum/T&T Clark, 2003. A fine theological analysis and critique of the way modern secular bioethics conceptualizes the human body can be found in G. P. McKenny, *To Relieve the Human Condition: Bioethics, Technology, and the Body*, State University of New York Press, 1997. A relatively brief, but lucid and theologically astute, overview of human genetic science is in R. Song, *Human Genetics: Fabricating the Future*, Pilgrim Press, 2002. The potentially deleterious consequences of genetic technologies for views of disability are examined from a number of different perspectives in J. Swinton and B. Brock, *Theology, Disability and the New Genetics: Why Science Needs the Church*, T&T Clark, 2007. A sustained and powerful theological critique of genetic reductionism and determinism can be found in T. Peters, *Playing God? Genetic Determinism and Human Freedom*, Routledge, 2003.

Notes

Preface: An Anglican gene? The lineage of this book

1   Ronald Preston, 'A Comment on Method', in Malcolm Brown and Peter Sedgwick (eds), *Putting Theology to Work*, CCBI and The William Temple Foundation, 1998, pp. 36–7.

2   Middle Axioms are emphatically not about 'splitting the difference' between opposing points of view. Rather, they seek a middle way between excessively general or vague pronouncements which cannot be translated into meaningful policy, and excessive specificity which not only appears to align God's will with detailed and fallible human programmes but tends to leave no room for legitimate disagreement between Christians as to the means by which good ends can be achieved. A good example of Middle Axioms can be found in the Appendix to Temple's *Christianity and Social Order* (1942), such as his principle that 'Every child should find itself a member of a family housed with decency and dignity . . . unspoilt by underfeeding or overcrowding . . .' This goes beyond the generalization that God wants children to flourish but stops short of saying (for example) that taxes should rise to pay for social housing. While this is close to the approach championed by Preston, he tended to avoid the term 'Middle Axiom', regarding it as misleading. I use the term here because it is a familiar expression for encapsulating Preston's methods.

3   Henry Clark, *The Church Under Thatcher*, SPCK, 1993, p. 1.

4   Francis Wheen, *How Mumbo-Jumbo Conquered the World: A Short History of Modern Delusions*, Fourth Estate, 2004.

5   See Michael Banner, 'Nothing to declare', *Church Times*, 16 June 1995.

6   John Atherton, *Marginalization*, SCM Press, 2003.

7   See Peter Sedgwick's rejoinder to Michael Banner, 'Refusing to despair over families', *Church Times*, 30 July 1995.

Chapter 1 Introduction: autonomy, solidarity and the human genome

1   This is not a bar to repeated challenges to their lawfulness and desirability on ethical and theological grounds. It might be said, counterculturally, that although lawyers and policy makers think that the basic questions were

discussed 20 years ago, they missed the point and the law should be radically changed.

2   Francis Crick (1916–2004) and James D. Watson (1928–) are popularly credited with the 'discovery' of the structure of DNA, although they relied heavily on the laboratory work of Maurice Wilkins (1916–2004), with whom they shared the Nobel Prize for Physiology or Medicine in 1962, and the underrated Rosalind Franklin (1920–58), who died tragically early.

3   Bishop Kallistos Ware writes, '[I]n the Jewish and Christian view, the human person is to be seen in thoroughly holistic terms: we are each of us, not a soul temporarily imprisoned in a body and longing to escape, but an integrated totality that embraces body and soul together.' K. Ware, *The Inner Kingdom*, St Vladimir, 2001, p. 30.

4   See A. Verhey, 'Mapping the human genome . . . biblically', in *Reading the Bible in the Strange World of Medicine*, Eerdmans, 2003, ch. 4.

5   274 US200 (1927).

6   J. Sulston and G. Ferry, *The Common Thread: Science, Politics, Ethics and the Human Genome*, Bantam Press, 2002, p. 270.

7   I. Kennedy and A. Grubb, *Medical Law*, 3rd edn, Butterworths, 2000.

8   D. Staniloae, *The Experience of God: Orthodox Dogmatic Theology. Vol. 2. The World, Creation and Deification*, Holy Cross Orthodox Press, 2005; C. Miller, *The Gift of the World: An Introduction to the Theology of Dumitru Staniloae*, T&T Clark, 2000, pp. 30–3.

Chapter 2 Applications of human genome information – case studies

1   Human Genome Project. http://www.ornl.gov/sci/techresources/ Human_Genome/home.shtml.

2   M. Cummings, *Human Heredity: Principles and Issues*, Bookes Cole, 2008.

3   Cummings, *Human Heredity*.

4   R. M. Ridley, C. D. Frith, T. J. Crow and P. M. Conneally, 'Anticipation in Huntington's Disease is inherited through the male line but may originate in the female', *Journal of Medical Genetics* 25, 1988, pp. 589–95; K. Kieburtz, M. MacDonald, C. Shih et al., 'Trinucleotide repeat length and progression of illness in Huntington's Disease', *Journal of Medical Genetics* 31, 1994, pp. 872–4.

5   Nuffield Council on Bioethics, *Mental Disorders and Genetics*, Nuffield Council on Bioethics, 1998. Also available at www.nuffieldbioethics.org.

6   C. Boyle and J. Savulescu, 'Ethics of using preimplantation genetic diagnosis to select a stem cell donor for an existing person', *British Medical Journal* 323, 2001, pp. 1240–3; G. Pennings, R. Schots and I. Lienaers, 'Ethical considerations on preimplantation genetic diagnosis for HLA typing to match a future child as a donor of haemopoietic stem cells to a sibling', *Human Reproduction* 17, 2002, pp. 534–8; S. Seldon and

S. Wilkinson, 'Should selecting saviour siblings be banned?', *Journal of Medical Ethics* 30, 2004, pp. 533–7.

7 D. M. Glitter, 'Am I my brother's keeper? The use of preimplantation genetic diagnosis to create a donor of transplantable stem cells for an older sibling suffering from a genetic disorder', *George Mason Law Review* 13, 2006, pp. 975–1035.

8 Human Fertilization and Embryology Authority, *Preimplantation tissue typing. Report of the preimplantation tissue typing policy review*, HMSO, 2004. Available from http://www.hfea.gov.uk/en/494.html.

9 S. Surendran, K. Michalis-Matalon, M. J. Quast, S. K. Tyring, J. Wei, E. L. Ezell and R. Matalon, 'Canavan Disease: a monogenic trait with complex genomic interaction', *Molecular Genetics and Metabolism* 80, 2003, pp. 74–80, erratum *Molecular Genetics and Metabolism* 87, p. 279; R. Matalon, K. Michalis-Matalon, S. Surendran and S. K. Tyring, 'Canavan Disease: studies on knockout mice', *Advances in Experimental Medicine and Biology* 576, 2006, pp. 77–93.

10 Nuffield Council on Bioethics, *The Ethics of Patenting DNA*, Nuffield Council on Bioethics, 2004. Also available at www.nuffieldbioethics.org.

11 N. Zamel, P. A. McClean, P. R. Sandell, K. A. Siminovitch and A. S. Slutsky, 'Asthma on Tristan da Cunha: looking for the genetic link', The University of Toronto Genetics of Asthma Research Group, *American Journal of Respiratory and Critical Care Medicine* 153, 1996, pp. 1902–6; L. J. Palmer and W. O. C. M. Cookson, 'Genomic approaches to understanding asthma', *Genome Research* 10, 2000, pp. 1280–7.

12 P. Heutink and B. A. Oostra, 'Gene finding in genetically isolated populations', *Human Molecular Genetics* 11, 2002, pp. 2507–15.

13 Nuffield Council on Bioethics, 'The forensic use of bioinformation: ethical issues', Cambridge Publishers Ltd, 2007. Also available at www.nuffieldbioethics.org.

14 M. Guillen, 'Ethical-legal problems of DNA databases in criminal investigation', *Journal of Medical Ethics* 26, 2000, pp. 266–71.

15 M. A. Jobling and P. Gill, 'Encoded evidence: DNA in forensic analysis', *Nature Reviews Genetics* 5, 2004, pp. 739–51.

16 M. K. Cho and P. Sankar, 'Forensic genetics and ethical, legal and social implications beyond the clinic', *Nature Genetics (Supp)* 36, 2004, s8–s12.

Chapter 3 The Bible and human genetics

1 Francis S. Collins, 'The Human Genome Project', in John F. Kilner, Rebecca D. Pentz and Frank E. Young (eds), *Genetic Ethics: Do the Ends Justify the Genes?*, Eerdmans, 1997, pp. 95–103 (95). For comment on this, see Allen Verhey, 'Mapping the Human Genome . . . biblically', in *Reading the Bible in the Strange World of Medicine*, Eerdmans, 2003, pp. 145–93 (159).

2 See further Richard B. Hays, *The Moral Vision of the New Testament: A Contemporary Introduction to New Testament Ethics*, T&T Clark, 1997, pp. 75–80.

3 Karl Barth, *Church Dogmatics*, vol. III, part 4, trans. A. T. Mackay et al., T&T Clark, 1961, p. 372.

4 For a good recent overview of the Bible's thinking in relation to the human embryo, see David Albert Jones, *The Soul of the Embryo: An Enquiry into the Status of the Human Embryo in the Christian Tradition*, Continuum, 2004, pp. 6–17, 43–56.

Chapter 4 The human genome and philosophical issues

1 Immanuel Kant, trans. James W. Ellington, *Grounding for the Metaphysics of Morals* [1785], 3rd edn, Hackett, 1993, p. 36.

2 John Locke, *Second Treatise of Government* [1690], ch. 5, section 27.

3 John Stuart Mill, *Three Essays: 'On Liberty', 'Representative Government', 'The Subjection of Women'*, Oxford University Press, 1975, ch. 1 in 'On Liberty'.

4 M. Spriggs, 'Lesbian couple create a child who is deaf like them', *Journal of Medical Ethics* 28.5, 2002, p. 283.

Chapter 5 The human genome and theological issues

1 James Randerson, 'Scientist plans to crack genetic secrets of the deep', *Guardian*, 14 March 2007, p. 9.

2 Francis S. Coline, in Ted Peters, *Playing God? Genetic Determinism and Human Freedom*, Routledge, 1977, p. ix.

3 Robert Song, *Human Genetics: Fabricating the Future*, Darton, Longman & Todd, 2002, pp. 10–14.

4 Gerald P. McKenny, *To Relieve the Human Condition: Bioethics, Technology, and the Body*, SUNY Press, 1997, p. 1.

5 Robert Song, 'The Human Genome Project as soteriological project', in Celia Deane-Drummond (ed.), *Brave New World: Theology, Ethics and the Human Genome*, Continuum/T&T Clark, 2003, p. 174. Cf. p. 178.

6 Peters, *Playing God?*, p. 11 (his italics).

7 Ruth Page, 'The human genome and the image of God', in Deane-Drummond (ed.), *Brave New World*, p. 77.

8 See Page, 'The human genome and the image of God', pp. 77–8.

9 Julie Clague, 'Beyond beneficence: the emergence of genomorality and the common good', in Deane-Drummond (ed.), *Brave New World*, p. 198.

10 *The Watchtower: announcing Jehovah's Kingdom*, vol. 128, no. 2, 15 January 2007, p. 3, italics added.

11 See Peter Manley Scott, 'The technological factor: redemption, nature and the image of God', *Zygon: Journal of Religion and Science* 35.2, June 2000, pp. 371–84, p. 376.

12 Bronislaw Szerszynski, 'That deep surface: the human genome project and the death of the human', in Deane-Drummond (ed.), *Brave New World*, p. 159.

13 Maureen Junker-Kenny, 'Genes and the self: anthropological questions to the Human Genome Project', in Deane-Drummond (ed.), *Brave New World*, p. 123.

14 Junker-Kenny, 'Genes and the self', p. 124.

15 Cited in Lisa Sowle Cahill, *Theological Bioethics: Participation, Justice, Change*, Georgetown University Press, 2005, p. 212.

16 Song, 'The Human Genome Project as soteriological project', p. 180.

17 Cahill, *Theological Bioethics*, p. 218.

18 Junker-Kenny, 'Genes and the self', p. 118–19.

19 Neil G. Messer, 'The Human Genome Project, health and the "tyranny of normality" ', in Deane-Drummond (ed.), *Brave New World*, pp. 103–7.

Chapter 7 Biotechnology patenting, ethics and theology

1 Audrey R. Chapman, *Unprecedented Choices: Religious Ethics at the Frontiers of Genetic Science*, Fortress Press, 1999, pp. 131–4 and references therein.

2 R. S. Crespi, 'Patents in biotechnology: the legal background', Proceedings of an International Conference on Patenting Life Forms in Europe, Brussels, 7–8/2/89, 1989, p. 7.

3 European Union, Directive 98/44/EC of the European Parliament and the Council, on the Legal Protection of Biotechnological Inventions, 6 July 1998, European Commission.

4 European Commission, 'Ethical aspects of patenting inventions involving elements of human origin, opinion of the group of advisors on ethical implications of biotechnology of the European Commission', 25 September 1996, European Commission.

5 The European Ecumenical Commission for Church and Society was an organization of European Protestant and Anglican churches in 15 countries, which in 1999 became the Church and Society Council of the Conference of European Churches (CEC), now also including Orthodox and Old Catholic churches. The EECCS Bioethics and Biotechnology Working Group has continued under the auspices of CEC.

6 See the European Ecumenical Commission for Church and Society documents: 'Critique of the draft EC patenting directive', September 1996; 'Clarification of the submission on the EC draft patenting directive from the

European Ecumenical Commission for Church and Society', 5 November 1996; 'Submission to the European Parliament on the "Common Position" of the draft directive on the patenting of biotechnological inventions', 28 March 1998; 'European Churches' group calls for urgent changes to patent directive: statement of European Ecumenical Commission for Church and Society', 30 April 1998; and D. M. Bruce, 'Whose genes are they? Genetics, patenting and the Churches', in C. Deane-Drummond (ed.), *Brave New World*, Continuum/T&T Clark, 2003.

7 David Hardy, *Human Genetic Engineering: Good or Evil?*, Methodist Publishing House, 1999.

8 Andrew Fox and Philip Challis (eds), *Making our Genes Fit: Christian Perspectives in the New Genetics*, Methodist Publishing House, 1999.

9 D. Bruce and A. Bruce (eds), *Engineering Genesis*, Earthscan, 1998, ch. 8.

10 See the Church of Scotland documents: *Ethical Concerns about Patenting in Relation to Living Organisms*, Reports of the Church of Scotland General Assembly, Edinburgh, 22 May 1997; *The Society, Religion and Technology Project Report on Genetically Modified Food*, Reports to the General Assembly and Deliverances of the General Assembly, 1999, pp. 20/93–20/103 and Board of National Mission Deliverances 42–5, 20/4; *The Society, Religion and Technology Project Report on GM Animals, Humans and the Future of Genetics*, Reports to the General Assembly and Deliverances of the General Assembly, 2001.

11 M. J. Reiss, 'Is it right to patent DNA?', *Bulletin of Medical Ethics*, January 1997, pp. 21–4; D. M. Bruce, 'Patenting human genes: a Christian view', *Bulletin of Medical Ethics*, January 1997, pp. 18–20.

12 Chapman, *Unprecedented Choices*, pp. 125–31, 156–60.

13 Geoff Tansey, *Trade, Intellectual Property, Food and Biodiversity: Key Issues and Options for the 1999 Review of Article 27.3(b) of the TRIPS Agreement*, Quaker Peace and Service, 1999; Carlos M. Correa, *Traditional Knowledge and Intellectual Property: A Discussion Paper*, Quaker Peace and Service, 2001.

14 Bob van Dillen and Maura Leen (eds), *Biopatenting and the Threat to Food Security: A Christian and Developmental Perspective*, CIDSE, 2000.

15 Article 53(a), European Patent Convention.

16 European Ecumenical Commission for Church and Society documents, 'Critique of the draft EC patenting directive'; 'Clarification of the submission on the EC draft patenting directive from the European Ecumenical Commission for Church and Society'; 'Submission to the European Parliament on the "Common Position" of the draft directive on the patenting of biotechnological inventions'; 'European Churches' group calls for urgent changes to patent directive: statement of European Ecumenical Commission for Church and Society'.

17 Bruce and Bruce (eds), *Engineering Genesis*, ch. 10.

18 European Patent EP 0 169 672, 'A Method for Producing Transgenic Animals', filed by The President and Fellows of Harvard College, 13 May 1992, originally filed as US Patent 662374, 22 June 1984.

19 European Ecumenical Commission for Church and Society documents, 'Critique of the draft EC patenting directive'; 'Clarification of the submission on the EC draft patenting directive from the European Ecumenical Commission for Church and Society'; 'Submission to the European Parliament on the "Common Position" of the draft directive on the patenting of biotechnological inventions'; 'European Churches' group calls for urgent changes to patent directive: statement of European Ecumenical Commission for Church and Society'.

20 Para. 51 of the preamble to the *Proposal for a European Parliament and Council Directive (EC) on the Legal Protection of Biotechnological Inventions*, 13 December 1995, COM(95) 661 final.

21 Nuffield Council on Bioethics, *The Ethics of Patenting DNA: A Discussion Paper*, Nuffield Council on Bioethics, 2002.

22 Conference of European Churches, *Human Stem Cell Patents would be Unethical: A Discussion Document of the Working Group on Bioethics Church and Society Commission*, Conference of European Churches, 2001.

23 European Patent Office, *Scenarios for the Future: How Might IP Regimes Evolve by 2025? What Global Legitimacy Might Such Regimes Have?* EPO Munich, 2007.

Chapter 8 The Church and the genomic project to secure the human future

1 *Gattaca* (1997), written and directed by Andrew B. Niccol.

2 See further Michael S. Northcott, 'In the waters of Babylon: the moral geography of the embryo', in Celia Deane-Drummond and Peter Manley Scott (eds), *Future Perfect? God, Medicine and Human Identity*, T&T Clark, 2006, pp. 73–86.

3 See also Aldous Huxley, *Brave New World*, Chatto & Windus, 1932; and Margaret Attwood, *Oryx and Crake*, Bloomsbury, 2003.

4 Barbara Rothman, *Genetic Maps and Human Imaginations: The Limits of Science in Understanding Who We Are*, W. W. Norton, 1998, pp. 109–10.

5 R. Myerowitz and F. C. Costigan, 'The major defect in Ashkenazi Jews with Tay-Sachs disease is an insertion in the gene for the alpha-chain of beta-hexosaminidase', *Journal of Biological Chemistry* 263, December 1988, pp. 185–9.

6 Rothman, *Genetic Maps and Human Imaginations*, pp. 118–19.

7 See Alec J. Jeffreys, John F. Y. Brookfield and Robert Semeonoff, 'Positive

identification of an immigration test-case using human DNA fingerprints', *Nature* 317, 31 October 1985, pp. 818–19.

8 In Christian just war theory it is not possible to declare war on anything that is not a nation-state. See further Michael Northcott, *An Angel Directs the Storm: Apocalyptic Religion and American Empire*, SCM Press, 2007.

9 Kristina Staley, *The Police National DNA Database: Balancing Crime Detection, Human Rights and Privacy*, Genewatch, 2005, and at http://www.genewatch.org/uploads/f03c6d66a9b354535738483c-1c3d49e4/NationalDNADatabase.pdf.

10 *Identity Cards Act*, HMSO, 2006, ch. 1, 5.5 c.

11 Francis S. Collins et al. suggest it is up to 'society' to formulate policy for the future forms of discrimination, enhancement and information storage that genomics will make possible. Francis S. Collins, Eric D. Green, Alan E. Guttmacher and Mark S. Guyer, 'A vision for the future of genomics research', *Nature* 422, 24 April 2003, pp. 835–47.

12 See especially Hans Jonas, *The Imperative of Responsibility: In Search of an Ethics for the Technological Age*, trans. Hans Jonas with David Herr, University of Chicago Press, 1984.

13 For an extended discussion of created order as a source of moral authority in the Christian tradition, see Michael S. Northcott, *The Environment and Christian Ethics*, Cambridge University Press, 1996.

14 See further Michael S. Northcott, *A Moral Climate: The Ethics of Global Warming*, Darton, Longman & Todd, 2007.

15 Michael Sandel, *The Case Against Perfection*, Belknap Press, 2007, p. 87.

16 Daniel T. Callahan, *The Troubled Dream of Life: Living with Mortality*, Simon and Schuster, 1990.

17 Sheldon Wolin insightfully suggests this tendency represents a new kind of inverted totalitarianism. S. Wolin, 'Inverted totalitarianism', *The Nation*, 19 May 2003 at http://www.thenation.com/doc/20030519/wolin.

18 President Bill Clinton, 'In his own words', cited in Rothman, *Genetic Maps and Human Imaginings*, p. 188.

19 See Oliver O'Donovan, *Begotten or Made?* Oxford University Press, 1984.

20 Sandel, *The Case Against Perfection*.

21 Ronald Dworkin, *Sovereign Virtue*, p. 452, cited in Sandel, *The Case Against Perfection*, pp. 76–7.

22 See Remi Brague's insightful comparison of autonomy and theonomy in Brague, *The Law of God*, trans. Lydia G. Cochrane, Chicago University Press, 2007.

23 Stanley Hauerwas, *The Peaceable Kingdom*, SCM Press, 1984, p. 106.

24 Rothman, *Genetic Maps and Human Imaginations*, p. 121.

25 See further John Howard Yoder, *The Politics of Jesus: Vicit Agnus Noster*, Eerdmans, 1972.

Chapter 9 A methodological interlude: a case for *rapprochement* between moral theology and moral philosophy

1 John Finnis and Germain Grisez include 'religion' among the basic human goods of which rational reflection on the ultimate reasons for action would make us aware. See J. Finnis, *Natural Law and Natural Rights*, Clarendon Press, 1980, pp. 89–90; and G. Grisez, *The Way of the Lord Jesus*, 3 vols, Vol. 1: *Christian Moral Principles*, Franciscan Herald Press, 1983, pp. 123–4. There are, of course, plenty of other, non-Roman Catholic philosophers who would dispute this.

2 See Nigel Biggar, *Aiming to Kill: The Ethics of Suicide and Euthanasia*, Darton, Longman & Todd, 2004, pp. 46–7.

3 As I myself found in relation to the sanguine views of liberal humanist philosophers such as Ronald Dworkin and Margaret Pabst Battin (*Aiming to Kill*, pp. 117, 158). I note, however, that whereas my view of the likely effects of legalizing intentional medical killing is distinctively pessimistic in comparison with these Anglo-Saxon philosophers, it is not so when compared with the views of a German philosopher such as Dieter Birnbacher ('Das Totungsverboten aus der Sicht des klassischen Utilitarismus', in Rainer Hegelsman and Reinhard Merkel (eds), *Zur Debatte über Euthanasie*, Suhrkamp Verlag, 1991, p. 42: 'Die zivilisatorische Decke is vielleicht dünner, als wir es uns träumen lassen . . .' ['the veneer of civilization is perhaps thinner than we allow ourselves to imagine']). I note that Jürgen Habermas shares a similar pessimism about the effects on society's moral common sense of normalizing the creation and destruction of embryos for the purpose of medical research and genetic engineering ('The debate on the ethical self-understanding of the species', in J. Habermas, *The Future of Human Nature*, Polity Press, 2003, pp. 20, 71–3, 94–5). I also note that the atheist Habermas acknowledges that the theological language of sin is better able to indicate the depths of evil than its secular equivalents ('Faith and knowledge', in *The Future of Human Nature*, p. 110).

4 As Svend Andersen implies when, writing of his experience on the Ethical Council of Denmark, he remarks that '[n]icht einmal mein theologischer Hintergrund war entscheidend' ['not once was my theological background decisive']. 'Die Rolle theologischer Argumentation im öffentlichen Leben', in Gotlind Ulshöfer (ed.), *Religion und Theologie im öffentlichen Diskurs: Hermeneutische und Ethische Perspektiven*, Arnoldshainer Texte 132, Haag & Herchen Verlag, 2005, p. 10.

5 Jeremy Waldron, *God, Locke, and Equality: Christian Foundations in Locke's Political Thought*, Cambridge University Press, 2002, p. 20.

6 Waldron's book is a rare exception that proves the rule: it argues for

the irreducibly theological nature of Locke's concept of basic human equality – and repeatedly suggests, with increasing volume, that such equality cannot be conceived *except* theologically. *God, Locke, and Equality*, pp. 82, 1, 48, 236, 13.

7 See Nigel Biggar, *The Hastening that Waits: Karl Barth's Ethics*, Oxford University Press, 1995, p. 159.

8 When I say 'non-theological ethical concepts', I do not mean to deny that ethical concepts in a moral theology are shaped by their theological environment. For example, a theology that affirms the morally conditional afterlife of individuals is likely to rate highly the importance of moral self-formation and therefore purity of intention, and it is unlikely to issue in a utilitarian ethic. Nevertheless, the question of whether or not a foreseen evil effect of a deliberately chosen act may reasonably be deemed unintended is one, I think, that can be adequately discussed without any reference to theological ideas.

9 Thus the witness of the philosopher Jeremy Waldron. For an instance of first-hand evidence, see Simon Blackburn, *Being Good*, Oxford University Press, 2001, pp. 10–19.

10 Jürgen Habermas, 'Habermas entre démocratie et génétique', *Le Monde*, 20 December 2002, p. viii: 'En ce qui concerne les questions fondamentales d'éthique politique, les voix religieuses ont au moins le même droit de se faire entendre dans l'espace public . . . C'est dans ce contexte d'une sécularisation qui "déraille" qu'il faut situer mon intérêt pour une approche respectueuse des traditions religieuses qui se distinguent par la capacité supérieure qu'elles ont d'articuler notre sensibilité morale.'

11 Jürgen Habermas, 'Faith and knowledge', in *The Future of Human Nature*, p. 109. 'Faith and knowledge' was first delivered as a lecture in October 2001.

12 Jeffrey Stout, *Democracy and Tradition*, Princeton University Press, 2004, pp. 10–11, 72–3, 79–80, 86–90.

13 Much hangs on what exactly it means to communicate 'responsibly', of course. But the general point is that no discussion can survive *any* kind of contribution. 'Fascist' tactics, be they physically or verbally violent, are designed to shut down dialogue and intimidate into conformity. If plural dialogue is to continue, therefore, it cannot be infinitely open. It must have limits. Some 'irresponsible' kinds of speech must be excluded – if need be, ironically, by force.

14 See note 13 immediately above.

Chapter 10 Conclusion: God, the 'whole' person and the human genome

1 N. Biggar, 'Saving the secular: the public vocation of moral theology'. An Inaugural Lecture delivered before the University of Oxford on 22 April 2008, p. 22 (downloaded and accessed 17 May 2008).

General index

Note: where more than one sequence of notes appears on the same page, notes are distinguished by the addition or a, b or c. Page references in **bold** type refer to Glossary entries.

ownership:
  of collective resource 51
  of genetic information 53–4
  and intellectual property 5, 17, 18,
    19–20, 27–9

Page, Ruth 72
Paris Convention (1883) 83
Patent Cooperation Treaty (1978) 83
patent law:
  and commerce 5, 6, 16, 19, 74–5,
    81–7
  history 82–5, 89
  and invention and discovery 84,
    91, 95–7, 99
  and social justice 98–100
patents 81, **130–31**
  and academic research 99, 101
  as exclusive rights 81, 86
  and intellectual property 81–2,
    88–9, 92, 93–5, 99, 100–101
  specifications 85–6
  see also gene patents
Perspectives in Economics xxii, xxvi,
  xxx
Peters, Ted 71
PGD *see* genetic diagnosis,
  pre-implantation
pharmacogenetics 8, **131**
physicalism 11, 12
PIGD *see* genetic diagnosis,
  pre-implantation
piracy, genetic 29
Plato 71
politics, consensual xvii, xx–xxi, xxiii
polymerase chain reaction 32, **131**
polypeptide chains 130, **131**
Preston, Ronald xviii, xxii, xxiii, xxiv
privacy:
  and DNA profiling 31
  and genetic information 18–19,
    53–4, 55–6
  as relational 18–19
property:
  collective 50, 54
  common 49–50, 54, 91, 97, 100
  in genetic material 46, 51–3, 54
  intellectual 1, 10, 16, 97, **130**
  and nature 94–5, 96

  and patents 81–2, 88–9, 92, 93–5,
    99, 100–101
  and private corporations 10, 16
  and Locke 18, 49–50, 51, 53, 54,
    74
  and ownership 5, 17, 18, 19–20,
    27–9, 46, 51, 53–4
  private 52, 53–4
proteins 8, 15, 20, 22, 129, **131**

Quakers (Society of Friends) 91

race, and genetic screening 103, 104
Rachels, James 117
Radical Orthodoxy xxiii–xxiv
Randerson, James 69, 138 n.1b
Rawls, John 118
Reagan, Ronald 111
reason, and ethics 116–19, 121
reductionism, genetic 15–16, 21, 22,
  56–7, 63–4, 75–6, 89, 115, 125
Reiss, M. J. 90
research ethics 52–3
resource:
  and commodity 46–9, 54
  as common property 49–50
  genetic material as 54
  human genome as 51–2, 54
responsibility, moral 106, 107, 110,
  117, 120
Rothman, Barbara 103, 104, 107–8,
  110

salvation, and healing 37–8, 40, 42
Sandel, Michael 106, 108
saviour siblings 15, 26–7, 126
science:
  privately-funded 10–11, 16
  social context 4, 114–15
  as value-laden 5
  see also technology, genetic
Scott, Peter Manley 2, 5, 15, 16, 17,
  66–80, 124
screening, genetic *see* genetic
  screening
sequencing 11, 23, 34, **132**
Sheppard, David xi, 124
sickle-cell anaemia 104, 105
sin, structural 67–8, 118

social ethics:
  and Anglicanism xvii–xxxi, 1–3,
    125
  and the Bible xxvii, 33–45
  and consensus xxviii–xxxi
  and gene patenting 88–101
  Middle Axiom approach xviii–xxiii,
    xxv–xxvi, xxix, 2
  and use of genetic materials 55
social justice 17, 19–20, 98–100
sociality 79–80
society:
  and change 70
  and individual 109–110
Society of Friends (Quakers) 91
Society, Religion and Technology
    Project (Church of Scotland) 90,
    94–5, 97, 100–101
solidarity 18–19, 78
  with created order 12, 21
  with humanity 4, 12, 17, 77, 108,
    110, 115, 127
Song, Robert xxvii, 4, 16, 33–45, 71,
    77, 124
species, boundaries 63, 106, 120
  and genetic reductionism 63–4
Staniloae, Dumitru 20–21
Statute of Monopolies (1623) 82
stem cell lines 100
Stout, Jeffrey 122–3
suffering:
  alleviation 4, 7, 11–12, 67, 69,
    111–13
  and idolatry of cure 4, 34, 38–40
  national and individual 37–8
suicide, physician-assisted 118
Sulston, Sir John 16, 100
surveillance 6, 103, 104–5, 107
Szerszynski, Bronislaw 75

Tansey, Geoff 91
Tay-Sachs disease 103–4, 105

technology, genetic:
  moral status 55–7
  and patent law 84–5
  as 'playing God' 14, 25, 46, 56–7,
    62, 71–2, 108, 120
  private companies 10–11, 16, 29,
    99, 100
  theological issues 66–80, 91–8
  uses 57–65
  as value-neutral 55
  and vision of the human 70–72,
    76, 78–80
  see also property, intellectual
Temple, William xvii–xviii, xix, xxiv,
    135 n.2
Thatcher, Margaret xx–xxi, xxii,
    111
theology *see* moral theology
therapy, and enhancement 12–13,
    43–5, 59–60
Trade-Related Aspects of
    Intellectual Property
    Rights Agreement (TRIPS)
    91

Universal Declaration on the Human
    Genome and Human Rights
    77
USA:
  and genetic screening 103–4
  and health inequalities 111

Venter, J. Craig 10, 16

Waldron, Jeremy 118–19, 143–4 n.6,
    144 n.9
Ware, Kallistos 136 n.3a
Watson, James D. 7, 10, 136 n.2a
Wheen, Francis xx
Wilkins, Maurice 136 n.2a
Winston, Robert 26
Wolin, Sheldon 142 n.17

Index of biblical references